TYNEHAM

A TRIBUTE

TYNEHAM
A TRIBUTE

DR ANDREW NORMAN

HALSGROVE

First published in Great Britain in 2007

Front cover picture: 'The Street', Tyneham, painted in watercolour by John Grant.

British Library Cataloguing-in-Publication Data
A CIP record for this title is available from the British Library

(Paperback) ISBN 978 1 84114 566 2
(Hardback) ISBN 978 1 84114 698 0

HALSGROVE
Halsgrove House
Ryelands Industrial Estate, Bagley Road,
Wellington, Somerset TA21 9PZ
Tel: 01823 653777
Fax: 01823 216796
email: sales@halsgrove.com
website: www.halsgrove.com

Printed and bound by
The Cromwell Press, Trowbridge

ABOUT THE AUTHOR

Andrew Norman was born in Newbury, Berkshire, UK in 1943. Having been educated at Thornhill High School, Gwelo, Southern Rhodesia (now Zimbabwe) and St Edmund Hall, Oxford, he qualified in medicine at the Radcliffe Infirmary. He has two children Bridget and Thomas, by his first wife.

From 1972-83, Andrew worked as a general practitioner in Poole, Dorset, before a spinal injury cut short his medical career. He is now an established writer whose published works include biographies of Thomas Hardy, TE Lawrence, Sir Francis Drake, Adolf Hitler, Agatha Christie, and Sir Arthur Conan Doyle. Andrew was remarried to Rachel in 2005.

All Andrew Norman's books are displayed on his website
www.andrew-norman.com

BOOKS BY THE SAME AUTHOR

(See Dr Andrew Norman's website www.andrew-norman.com)

Adolf Hitler: The Final Analysis (Spellmount)

Agatha Christie: The Finished Portrait (Tempus)

Arthur Conan Doyle: Beyond Sherlock Holmes (Tempus)

By Swords Divided: Corfe Castle in the Civil War (Halsgrove)

Dunshay: Reflections on a Dorset Manor House (Halsgrove)

Enid Blyton and her Enchantment with Dorset (Halsgrove)

HMS Hood: Pride of the Royal Navy (Stackpole Books)

Robert Mugabe and the Betrayal of Zimbabwe (McFarland & Co.)

Sir Francis Drake: Behind the Pirate's Mask (Halsgrove)

TE Lawrence: Unravelling the Enigma (Halsgrove)

Thomas Hardy: Behind the Inscrutable Smile (Halsgrove)

Thomas Hardy: Christmas Carollings (Halsgrove)

CONTENTS

ACKNOWLEDGEMENTS

I am indebted to many former residents of the Parish of Tyneham-cum-Steeple for the sharing of their reminiscences and the loan of photographs. My special thanks go to Major General HMG Bond, Helen Taylor, Margot Bond, George and Sylvia (née House) Braisby, Joseph Dando, Kathleen and Cyril Barnes, Mabel Taylor, Joan Brachi, Jenny Elmes, Ione Heath (née Ware), Meg Kingston (née Ritchie), and Arthur Grant. Also to Winnie Applin, George Willey, John Ritchie, Bridget Dixon (née Sheasby), Tim Ware, Dr Philip Mansel, John Mayes, David Haysom, and Julie Astin.

My thanks also to the Dorset County Museum; Dorset County Archivist; Tony Ellis (Archivist), and Angela Fisher (Assistant Archivist) of the Maritime Coastguard Agency at Bridlington. Also to Brian Wead of the RNLI Poole; the staff of Poole Library and Poole Local Studies Library; Dovecote Press for permission to refer to material in Lilian Bond's book *Tyneham, A Lost Heritage*; Dorset Archives Service for permission to reproduce an entry from the *Tyneham Marriage Register* of 1943; Range Liaison Officer Mick Burgess of Lulworth Range Control, and Range Controller and staff at the Photographic Section, Royal Armoured Corps, Bovington for supplying archive material and for permission to use official photographs; finally, to John Howard Waldin for producing the maps of Tyneham, Tyneham House and Worbarrow.

I am especially grateful to my dear wife Rachel for all her help and encouragement.

PREFACE

Like many visitors to the now largely ruined village of Tyneham, I was led to wonder what circumstances had led to its decline, and ask myself what life was really like when this was a living, breathing, and vibrant community. The answer came in a quite unexpected way, when in August 1986, I happened to meet Miss Helen Taylor, formerly seamstress at Tyneham House; also her elder sister Elizabeth, known as 'Bessie'. At that time they were living at Corfe Castle – having been evicted from Tyneham, along with all the other villagers, in December 1943.

When Miss Taylor allowed me to make a voice recording of her reminiscences, this was just prior to her 85th birthday, when Bessie was aged 94. I immediately thought to myself what a wonderful story this would make. It is surely too good to waste; not only from the point of view of entertainment, but also for the historical record that it provides.

I was also fortunate to meet, and receive assistance from General Mark Bond, whose father Ralph was the last owner of Tyneham House. He (General Bond) provided details of life 'upstairs', as it were, as opposed to 'downstairs'.

By a strange coincidence, Miss Taylor spent her declining years in a nursing home in Swanage which I happened to own. Here, she kindly elaborated on many of the fascinating stories which she had told me on our first meeting. I now set to work on my book, which I hope my readers will enjoy as much as I have enjoyed writing it.

A youthful Helen Taylor with dog, 'Spot'. Photo: Helen Taylor

1

THE BOMBSHELL

It was Charlie Beauchamp, the postmaster at Creech village away over the hill from Tyneham, who delivered the news in the form of a sack full of brown, official looking envelopes, one of which he posted through the door of every household. There were no numbers on the doors of the houses in Tyneham village. Neither the post office, nor the villagers had any need of them; for the postman knew everyone personally, by name. The letter read as follows:

> In order to give our troops the fullest opportunity to perfect their training in the use of modern weapons of war, the Army must have an area of land particularly suited to their special needs, and in which they can use live shells. For this reason you will realize the chosen area must be cleared of all civilians.
>
> The most careful search has been made to find an area suitable for the Army's purpose and which, at the same time, will involve the smallest number of persons and property. The area decided on, after the most careful consultation between the Government authorities concerned, lies roughly inside the square formed by EAST LULWORTH – EAST STOKE – EAST HOLME – KIMMERIDGE BAY.
>
> It is regretted that, in the National Interest, it is necessary to move you from your homes, and everything possible will be done to help you, both by payment of compensation, and by finding other accommodation for you if you are unable to do so yourself.
>
> The date on which the Military will take over this area is the 19th December next, and all civilians must be out of the area by that date.
>
> The Government appreciate that this is no small sacrifice that you are asked to make but they are sure that you will give this further help towards winning the war with a good heart.

It was signed CH Miller, Major General i/c Administration, Southern Command, and signed 16th November, 1943 (today being the 17th). For the residents of Tyneham, the most significant part of the letter, which was in fact an Eviction Order, was the phrase, written in longhand (not typed, like the remainder), 'including your properties – see overleaf.' The Order also applied to the hamlets of West Creech, Povington, Worbarrow, Baltington, North and South Egliston, and Lutton.

As if this were not enough, the villagers had another problem to contend with, for the winter of 1943 was a particularly cold one. Most of whom had known no other home. Now they were to be scattered far and wide; yet they held in their hearts the hope that one day they would be permitted to return to their beloved Tyneham. After all, World War II, which had been in progress since 3 September 1939, presumably could not go on forever. The Allied victories at El Alamein (October/November 1942), Stalingrad (February 1943) and the Allied invasion of Sicily (September 1943) meant that the tide had already turned in their favour.

Before she left, Helen Taylor, one of the residents who happened to be the last to leave, pinned a note onto the door of Tyneham's Church of St Mary the Virgin:

Please treat the church and houses with care. We have given up our homes where many of us lived for generations to help win the war to keep men free. We shall return one day and thank you for treating the village kindly.

She was aged 42 at the time. The total number of villagers evicted was around 225, with 40 of these coming from Tyneham itself.

SLA/7155/R Army Form A.2016.

NOTICE OF TAKING OF POSSESSION OF LAND UNDER THE PROVISIONS OF REGULATION 51 OF THE DEFENCE REGULATIONS, 1939.

North Cottage, Orchard Cottages, Tenant: P. Taylor.
West Creech, Steeple, Dorset.

To the owner and occupier of the land and buildings described in the Schedule hereto annexed.

I,* Colonel [illegible] R. Kennedy, being one of a class of persons to whom the Secretary of State as a competent authority for the purposes of Part IV of the Defence Regulations, 1939, has in exercise of the powers contained in that Part of the said Defence Regulations delegated the necessary authority, give notice that I, on behalf of the Secretary of State, take possession of the land and buildings described in the Schedule hereto annexed.

(Signed) [illegible] Capt.
for Officer i/c Administration, Southern Command.

Date 6th January, 1944.
w.e.f 17th November, 1943.

I hereby acknowledge receipt of a notice of which the above is a duplicate.

(Owner).
P. Taylor (Occupier).

*Rank and name of M.G.A. or Senior Administrative Officer of the Command Corps District or District must be inserted here.

N.B.—A plan or full description of the property to be annexed.

This form will be made out in triplicate—(a) original for owner or occupier; (b) duplicate, signed by party dispossessed for Command Land Agent's local representative; and (c) triplicate signed by party dispossessed for S.A.O.C.

This form must NOT be used for requisitioning chattels.

The Possession Order. Photo: John Mayes

2

THE PARISH

The village of Tyneham lay in a lush green valley, within a mile of the sea, in a remote area on the south coast of Dorset. To the north was Grange Hill, Whiteway Hill, and Povington Hill, from where the white cliffs of Arish Mell could be seen, with the Mupe Rocks stretching out into the sea. To the south was the still higher peak of Tyneham Cap, and Gad Cliff, whose jagged edge could be seen silhouetted against the sky, with Brandy Bay beyond. A path, running south westwards to the sea, ended at Worbarrow Bay from where, on a clear day, the long, squat Isle of Portland could be seen away to the west.

Povington Hill is of historical interest because here are to be found twenty late Bronze Age and early Iron Age 'barrows' (dome-shaped burial chambers): the largest one measuring 65 yards in diameter. Here, bodies

Tyneham village: Street, Row and Church.
Photo: Crown copyright

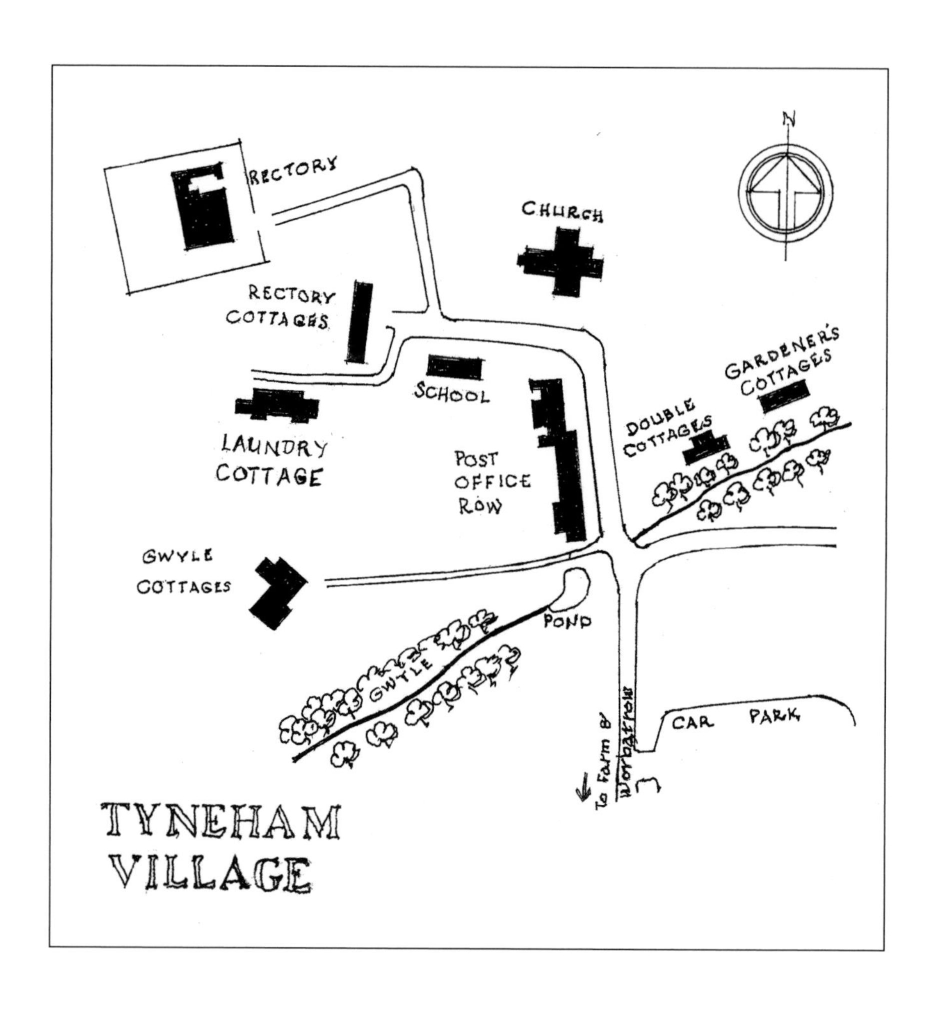
N
RECTORY
CHURCH
RECTORY
COTTAGES
SCHOOL
LAUNDRY
COTTAGE
POST
OFFICE
ROW
DOUBLE
COTTAGES
GARDENER'S
COTTAGES
GWYLE
COTTAGES
POND
GWYLE
To Farm &
Worbarrow
CAR PARK
TYNEHAM
VILLAGE

were buried in a curled up, foetal position; a drinking vessel being placed at the head in order to sustain the soul of that person on his or her journey to the afterlife. The largest barrow was, presumably, built for a local chieftain. The rectangular outlines of the fields on the slopes of nearby Gold Down and Whiteway Hill, indicate that these were probably of Celtic origin (i.e. pre-Roman).

At 600 feet above sea level, the most spectacular man-made feature in the region is Flowers Barrow: an Iron Age fort, towering over Worbarrow Bay with commanding views of the English Channel. When the Romans arrived, they established themselves here, and it is believed that the name 'Flower' derives from the name of a Roman officer named 'Florus'.

The Celtic tribe Dwr y Triges – 'the people who live near the tidal water' manufactured amulets (ornaments used as charms against evil) out of the soft, friable shale stone which is found at nearby Kimmeridge. The amulets were made on primitive lathes and polished until they shone

Working in the fields (prior to the Great War): standing, the Tizzards, including Frank and Alfred; seated, left to right, Bert Taylor, Fred Lucas, Frank Gould, Charlie Meech (with 'Daniel'), and Shepherd Lucas. Photo: Helen Taylor

with a black lustre. They were worn either as bracelets, or as part of a necklace. When in 1839, a Roman cemetery was excavated at Dorchester, the skeleton of a female was discovered with an amulet still attached to her wrist; indicating that the Romans continued to produce these objects after their invasion of Britain in the 1st Century AD. According to 18th Century Dorset historian the Reverend John Hutchins, there were manufactuaries for amulets at both Povington and Kimmeridge.

In more recent times (as Lilian Bond pointed out in her charming and informative book *Tyneham – a Lost Heritage*, published in 1956), the people of that part of Dorset had a vocabulary of their own. For example: faggots, carried home by hedgers at the end of their working day were known as '*nitches*'; when a fisherman talked of the weather being '*caffety*', he meant that it was unsettled; a '*drong*' was a narrow, closed-in lane or passage; a son was called '*zon*' or '*zonny*', and a daughter my little '*meaid*' or '*meaden*'. Layering was known locally as '*plashing*' or '*plushing*'.

3

THE CHURCH

Situated at the top of Tyneham's one and only road, known as 'The Street' (with its line of terraced houses known as 'The Row') was the mediaeval church of St Mary the Virgin, whose first rector (according to the plaque on the wall) was Thomas de Kingston, who resigned from his post on 1 February 1303. In 1721, when the Reverend Bernard Toupe was rector, the Parish of Tyneham (3,000 acres) was united with that of nearby Steeple by Act of Parliament, and thus became the Parish of Tyneham-cum-Steeple.

In the 18th and 19th Centuries, it was the local landowning Bond family who provided Tyneham Church's rectors: three of whom put in no less than 147 successive years of service. They were Denis Bond (1742-

The Church of St Mary the Virgin, Tyneham. Photo: Crown Copyright

Mrs Frend, the rector's wife, and her niece at the Rectory. Photo: Crown copyright

1795), William Bond (1795-1852), and Nathaniel Bond of Grange (1852-1889). (It is interesting to note that in the remaining fifty-four years of Tyneham church's ecclesiastical life – i.e. up until 1943 – no less than seven rectors came and went).

Everyone was required to attend church: the Bond family of Tyneham House being admitted through a separate entrance from the rest of the villagers, and having their own pews. In fact, with the increasing population, a south transept was added to the church in 1840, to contain new pews installed for the use of the Bond household.

Prior to 1848, Divine Service was performed in the parish on each Sunday of the year, and also on Ash Wednesday, Good Friday, and Christmas Day. However, in that year, the Reverend William Bond gave the sum of £1,700 to the governors of Queen Anne's Bounty (tax payable to the Crown by the clergy on income from their livings, established in

1704) on trust, to pay the dividends half yearly to the rector of Tyneham, on condition that two full services, with a sermon, were performed every Sunday and also on Good Friday and Christmas Day.

On the west side of the church lay the rectory, built in 1876, from which excellent views could be obtained - down the Tyneham Valley to Baltington Farm with the sea beyond, and the ramparts of Flowers Barrow silhouetted against the skyline. Canon Christopher Wordsworth, who became rector in 1889, intended to take full advantage of this view, by felling the line of fir trees which had been deliberately planted to provide a wind-break against the gales and even hurricanes, which occasionally ravaged the coast. As a result, in such conditions, the house shook, terrifying the family, including his wife and nine children.

In his latter years, Helen Taylor's father William, the woodman of Tyneham, was appointed Parish Clerk and Sexton by the Bond family. His responsibilities included lighting the church's oil lamps and candles (there being no electricity); keeping the 'tortoise' wood-burning stove burning, and ringing the bells (of which there were two) for services. They were also rung if there was a death in the Valley. On Sundays, the brass eagle on the lectern and the gleaming altar cross were polished until they shone. It was Helen's task to sweep the steps, prior to the service.

On Good Friday, the village children, escorted by the Bonds' daughters, went to the woods to pick primroses and bluebells with which to decorate the church; tying them up in bunches with lengths of wool and carrying them in their wicker baskets. After the Easter Day service, everyone was given a penny and a hot cross bun by Mrs Bond. The remainder of the day was taken as a holiday, which the menfolk would spend in their gardens, observing the time-honoured tradition of planting out their potato crops. At Harvest Festival the Bonds sent flowers, fruit and vegetables, grown in the gardens of Tyneham House, to the Church. Once again, the children gathered wild flowers and made them into posies to decorate the font and the window-sills; whereas the rectory servants were responsible for the floral decoration of the pulpit and lectern. This was the occasion for the children to be presented with

Sylvia House and George Braisby on their wedding day. Photo: Sylvia and George Braisby

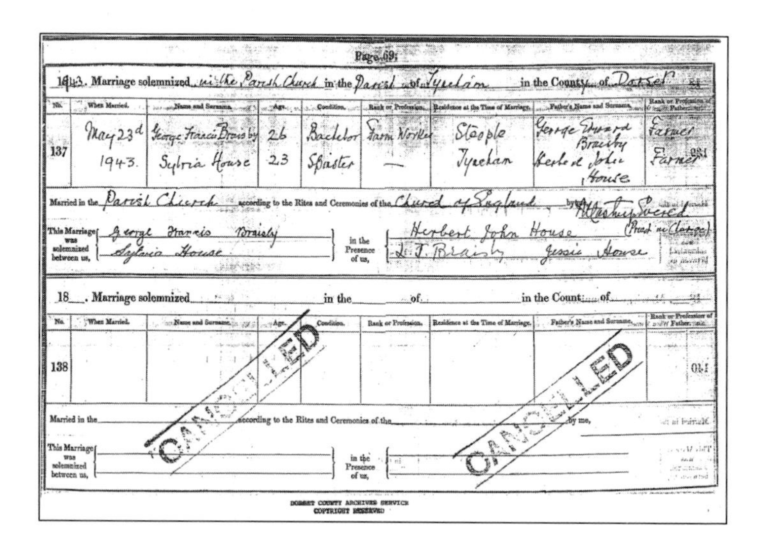

Page 69.

1943. Marriage solemnized in the Parish Church in the Parish of Tyneham in the County of Dorset

No.	When Married.	Name and Surname.	Age.	Condition.	Rank or Profession.	Residence at the Time of Marriage.	Father's Name and Surname.	Rank or Profession of Father.
137	May 23d 1943.	George Francis Braisby	26	Bachelor	Farm Worker	Steeple	George Edward Braisby	Farmer
		Sylvia House	23	Spinster	—	Tyneham	Herbert John House	Farmer

Married in the Parish Church according to the Rites and Ceremonies of the Church of England by me, [illegible]

This Marriage was solemnized between us, George Francis Braisby, Sylvia House

in the Presence of us, Herbert John House (Priest in Charge), L. T. Braisby, Jessie House

18__. Marriage solemnized ___ in the ___ of ___ in the County of ___

No.	When Married.	Name and Surname.	Age.	Condition.	Rank or Profession.	Residence at the Time of Marriage.	Father's Name and Surname.	Rank or Profession of Father.
138								

Married in the ___ according to the Rites and Ceremonies of the ___ by me,

This Marriage was solemnized between us, ___ in the Presence of us, ___

CANCELLED CANCELLED

DORSET COUNTY ARCHIVES SERVICE
COPYRIGHT RESERVED

prizes for 'good attendance' at school and at Sunday School, and for 'good answering in the Bible and Prayer Book'. Sunday School played an important part in the lives of the village children, and in Helen's time, having attended Sunday School herself, she eventually became a teacher, along with Cicely, Margot and Lilian, the younger members of the Bond family. At Christmastime, the very finest gold-embossed altar cloth was brought into use.

On 23 May 1923, Sylvia House of Povington Farm, who taught at Tyneham Sunday School, married George Francis Braisby of Blackmanston Farm, Steeple. On that occasion, Helen Taylor made a daisy chain and looped it across the handrail, so that as the newly-wed couple came down the steps after the service, they broke it. Little did the villagers know, that this would be the last wedding ever to take place at Tyneham Church.

4
THE SCHOOL

Tyneham School was established in the year 1860 by the Reverend Nathaniel Bond (kinsman of the Bonds of Tyneham, and Rector of Tyneham Church from 1852 to 1889) of nearby Grange. In May 1872, under the heading 'Tyneham National School, Dorset, Wareham and Isle of Purbeck Poor Law Union' (Poor Law – English system for poor relief, established by the Poor Law Relief Act, 1601), he gave the following description of the school and its origins:

> The Building is private property, erected on the Glebe belonging to the Rectory of Tyneham (not leased). The School [is] managed by the Rev. N Bond, Rector [i.e. himself] and Rev. William Truell, Curate of Tyneham without any written Regulations.

(The Truell family, incidentally, were related to the Bonds). There then followed details of the construction and dimensions of the schoolroom and the availability of light.

> Boys, Girls, Infants, same management, [and all within] same building. Present School Buildings erected A.D. 1860 (from materials of old Tithe Barn).
>
> Income (for year ending July 1, 1871):

Voluntary contributions (£)	31–5-0
School Pence	7-0-0
	38-5-0
Expenditure	
Teacher (£)	25- 0-0
Assistant	4- 0-0
Books, aprons	3- 5-0
Fuel, light	4-10-0
Repairs	1-10-0
	38- 5-0

The weekly rates for pupils were listed as: twopence per pupil, or three-pence per family. The numbers of pupils in attendance were as follows: boys six, girls seventeen, infants fifteen: total thirty-eight. The number of prospective pupils who had accepted the offer of free education from 1st September 1891-97 was eighty-two.

The school - which took children up to the age of 14 and from all parts of the parish, consisted of a single large room, where the pupils had their lessons. The infants occupied a platform at the far end, which was screened off by a curtain. In Helen Taylor's time, it was on this platform that the dentist would set up his dreaded pedal-driven drill, when he made his periodic visits to the school. Heating was provided by a 'tortoise' wood-burning stove (similar to the one in the church). In wet weather, the children would hang their soggy clothes on its large fireguard, in order to dry them out. It also had a ledge upon which wet boots could be placed. (Most children possessed only a single pair of boots, but the more well-to-do had a pair for weekdays, and a pair of shoes for Sundays).

The class of 1912 in their 'Sunday Best' (Helen Taylor top left). Photo: Julie Astin

When Helen Taylor was a pupil at the school (1907-16), Miss Norah Woodman was Head Teacher. She occupied the northern-most cottage of a terrace facing The Street. (These cottages were known as 'Post Office Row' - or simply as 'The Row'). Between the cottage and the school was the playground, with a fence and gate to keep out farm animals. Miss Woodman's assistant Miss Gladys Wright (who was also her niece), had charge of the infants. At school, children were taught the basic skills, but due to Tyneham's rural situation, the emphasis was very much on nature studies and nature walks.

In the school photograph of 1912, Miss Woodman's niece (who taught the infants) is depicted, but not Miss Woodman herself. Helen Taylor declared that this was because Miss Woodman refused to have her photograph taken, on the grounds that she had 'a bad [i.e. un-photogenic] nose'.

Above the fireplace hung a large portrait of the late King, Edward VII, who on his death in 1910, was succeeded by George V. Beneath it was displayed a poem which Helen Taylor had composed herself, and written out in her best handwriting:

Lost – several golden moments
between sunrise and sunset.
No reward is offered,
as they are gone forever.

The fees for attending school had remained unchanged since the time when the Reverend Nathaniel Bond made his report in 1871. However, the funds raised in this way were insufficient to pay Miss Woodman's salary of £25 per annum, and that of Miss Wright, £4 per annum; to say nothing of the cost of fuel, lighting and books. All these expenses had to be supplemented by voluntary contributions.

Some of the children had to walk several miles to school. Kathy Wrixon for example, lived at Povington Farm with her parents and her four brothers. Sometimes, in the winter when the gales blew and the snow lay on the ground, the children were *shrammed* (the local word for frozen) with cold, and little Billy Wrixon would have to hang on to farm fences to avoid being blown away. As Povington Hill was 600 feet in height, the return journey was extremely arduous.

At 9 a.m., the entire school assembled in the playground in a long line, to await the arrival of the rector the Reverend Claude Homan. The school's largest boy or girl was chosen to stand by the front door, holding the Union Jack on a flagpole, as everyone marched around saluting the flag in turn. After this, there would be hymns, prayers, and a scripture lesson taken by the rector, who would then be available should Miss Woodman require any extra help in the classroom. At break-time, water was heated up on the stove; then cocoa powder and sugar (supplied by the children themselves) were added and the concoction was drunk from enamel mugs. Those who lived nearby went home for lunch; others, from further afield, remained on the premises and ate the sandwiches which they had brought with them. There was no homework: this was not considered necessary, as all work was done during the school day. Miss Wright dispensed discipline by rapping a boy (or girl) across the knuckles with her ruler. However, rather than see any of her charges go hungry, she would purchase potatoes and the ingredients to make soup, with her own money.

As the pupils were mainly the offspring of farm labourers, there was a certain amount of coming and going when a family moved to work on another farm. If a child's parents were fortunate enough to be employed at Tyneham House or on the Tyneham Estate, however, then those parents could usually be sure of having a 'job for life'.

Absenteeism from school was often a problem, not usually due to truancy, but simply because the gales, blizzards and snow drifts of winter made life impossible, particularly for those pupils who had to walk, say, a mile from the village of Lutton, or the 2 miles from Steeple; to say nothing of those who had to cross northern hills. Miss Woodman was obliged to report these absences to the Attendance Officer, but in the circumstances there was little that could be done. Another reason for absence from school was illness. For example, when Helen Taylor's brother Bert caught diphtheria, both she and her sister Betty were kept at home for fear of passing it on. Judy, Maggie and Daisy Warr were excluded from school by Nurse Jones for having 'verminous heads'; as was Evelyn Longman when she developed impetigo – Dr Drury advising her to stay at home until the scabs had cleared. When the unfortunate Maggie developed a discharge from her ear, Mrs Bond of Tyneham House arranged and paid for her to spend 3 weeks of convalescence by the sea at Swanage, in the hope that the change of air might do her good. A pupil might also be absent when he or she had to make an emergency visit to the dentist at Corfe Castle; or go to Wool to attend a confirmation class. Tom Everett and Harry Matthews were always excused school in September, when they had to help their families with the harvest.

The school's Diocesan Inspector EJ Tadman reported on Tyneham School in glowing terms:

> The teaching is thorough and the children
> answer brightly and thoughtfully. The school
> is in excellent order. The results, on the
> whole, are in advance of last year's. The
> quiet, reverent tone is very pleasing....'

Empire Day, circa 1900. Photo: Helen Taylor

When His Majesty's Inspector of Schools came to visit, he too must have formed the same impression; for afterwards the children were given the rest of the day off as a half holiday! In the event, they were all taken down to the seashore at Worbarrow in a horse-drawn wagon, to be joined there for tea by the Sunday School children and members of the choir.

Empire Day – 24 May – was another important occasion when the children were reminded of their responsibilities to their country, and of the fact that they were citizens of a glorious empire which stretched right around the world. The Union flag was raised on the grassy knoll outside Miss Taylor's home 'Laundry Cottage'; although Miss Woodman said another site might have to be chosen for the ceremony, because the cows would keep knocking the flagpole over!. That afternoon, the children were awarded another half holiday.

5

TYNEHAM FARM

On the south side of the village was Tyneham Farm - part of the Bond Estate – and, in Miss Taylor's time, leased by the eccentric Walter Case Smith. Farmer Smith's nickname was 'Leather Jacket' because he was invariably to be seen wearing a leather jacket. This was a mixed farm – arable with livestock including cows, pigs, and heavy horses for ploughing. Each heavy horse had a name, such as 'Mary', 'Duke', 'Captain' and 'Violet'.

Other farms in the area were Baltington (further down the Valley), Steeple Leaze (further up), and Whiteway, Povington, and West Creech over the hill to the north.

On Thursdays, lambs, calves and pigs were transported by cart to the village of Wool, from there to be taken by train to Dorchester to be sold at the market. A milk cart transported milk from the Tyneham

The Tyneham Valley. Photo: Sylvia Braisby

Farmer Walter Case Smith at Tyneham Farm, with 20hp Austin tourer. Photo: Crown copyright

Worbarrow Bay and 'Tout' (conical hill). Photo: Helen Taylor

Tom Mintern. Photo: Helen Taylor

Valley to Corfe Castle, from where it was sent by train to London. In his dairy, Farmer Smith kept a supply of salted fish – caught locally at Worbarrow – which he sold to the villagers. After World War I, he purchased a new Austin 20 Tourer; this was his pride and joy.

On the hill above Worbarrow Bay, stood a cottage where small-holder Tom Mintern lived with his wife Sarah, three daughters and son William ('Billy'). Billy subsequently lost his life, aged 16, when he and another boy, who was visiting from London, went out together in a small boat and were drowned off the headland at the tip of Worbarrow Tout, known as The Point (neither boy being able to swim).

Tom, whose heifers and cows were to be seen grazing the lush green grass of Worbarrow Tout (a conical hill situated on the east side of the bay) delivered one pint of milk, every morning and every evening, to each village household. At the side of his cottage was a small annexe where Sarah made the butter. Tom's assistant was Jimmy Presley, who considered himself to be something of an evangelist, and delivered not only the milk, but also quotations from the Bible!

The house at the south end of The Row was occupied by Shepherd Lucas, his wife, and their sheepdog Sam. In the former's charge were 700 or so sheep, mainly of the Dorset Horn variety (which have the ability to breed all year round, and not just in springtime), but there were also some 'Shropshires', which had been introduced to Tyneham by the Reverend Nathaniel Bond of Grange. Each sheep had a bell hung around its neck, and from the sound of their notes, the shepherd could tell whether his animals were contented or agitated, perhaps by the presence of a lurking fox, or a scavenging seagull.

Shepherd Lucas was at his busiest in springtime, when he was on duty, day and night, for the lambing. At night, having first made sure that his sheep were safe and sound in their hurdle-pens, he would sleep in the back of a small, covered wagon, which had wheels so that it could be hauled from place to place by a pony, as the need arose. June was another busy time, when the flock was shepherded down into the village for shearing in the barn by a band of hired 'journeymen' shearers (scissor-shaped clippers being used in those days).

In former times, a great sheep fair was held regularly at Woodbury Hill, 10 miles away to the north. This was also a great social event, with fortune-tellers and horse traders in evidence. There were swings, helter-skelters and steam-driven roundabouts; also 'peep' shows, where such legendary tales as *Dick Turpin's Ride to York* and *The Death of Black Beauty* were re-enacted; a refreshment tent where tea, coffee, plum pudding and 'furmity' (wheat boiled with eggs and spices and laced with rum) was served. (Such a scene was described by the Dorset author Thomas Hardy in his novel *The Mayor of Casterbridge*).

In those days, the tracks or roads ran across the fields, which were separated from each other by 'barways' (barriers made by setting two tall stone posts into the ground on either side of the road, with planks which were then slipped down into grooves cut into their sides). The fields had delightful names which often denoted their use: East and West Corn Ground, Lower Horse Close, Calves House Ground, Rook Grove, Higher Westfield, Eweleaze and West Eweleaze, North Cowleaze, Old Cowleaze, and Lower Cowleaze ('leaze' being the Dorset name for pasture).

Life on the farm could be extremely arduous. Mabel Cake of West Creech Farm used to take it in turns with her sister Violet, to get up at 4.30 a.m. to help milk the cows - even though she was still a schoolgirl. Farm life was also not without its dangers. Sylvia, daughter of Jessica and Herbert House of Povington Farm for example, used to run errands to Tyneham Post Office for her mother. This involved a bicycle ride to the top of Grange Hill, from where she could free-wheel all the way down to the bottom. One day, however, she ran straight into a herd of Farmer Smith's cows, which wandered freely, there being no fences to keep them in. She sought refuge behind the bramble bush, and could only watch as the bull, which accompanied them, sniffed at her bicycle, and then proceeded to lick it all over before going on his way. She considered that she had had a narrow escape. In fact, whereas a bull on its own can be a dangerous and unpredictable creature, one in a field of cows is seldom a problem. Not every farm was able to afford a bull; so at the appropriate time, a travelling bull was hired and transported round the whole area by horse and cart.

The itinerant bull. Photo: Mark Bond

6
GEORGE RICHARDS

George Richards had been a farm labourer all his life, and he was the last person in Tyneham to wear a smock. Smocks were made of flax: a hard-wearing material which would also keep the wearer dry in all weathers. Embroidered on the front were patterns denoting the owner's occupation. For example, on a shepherd's smock – crooks, hurdles, and lambs might be portrayed. Those who were well-to-do had one smock for weekdays and another for Sunday best.

In his later years, George, who always rose at the crack of dawn, became increasingly absent-minded in that he would forget what day of the week it was. He was, therefore, often to be seen out in the fields on a Sunday – the day of rest – hoeing the turnips and swedes; or when the cattle had devoured the tops of the turnips, grubbing them up by the roots with a hooked tool called a 'hacker', so that they could then consume the bottom half and nothing would be wasted. George had no intention of retiring. No pension was provided in those days, and Parish Relief would have given him a mere half a crown per week, when at the time, a large loaf of bread cost fourpence, a small loaf twopence, butter a shilling a pound, a pair of shoes 2s 11d, and a good pair of working boots 4s 11d.

As he lived on his own he did not know Sundays from weekdays, and Helen Taylor would be sent up to tell him it was Sunday and that he must go home. Finally, George's sister Mrs Manktelow came to live with him and look after him.

George Richards, farm labourer, with sister Mrs Manktelow. Photo: Helen Taylor

7

THE FISHERMEN

A footpath, alongside the Gwyle Stream (pronounced 'goyle' – meaning wooded glen with stream running through it) led to Worbarrow Bay, home to a small community of fishermen: all of whose surname was 'Miller'. The Millers had allegedly sailed down from Scotland at some unknown date and landed on the Dorset coast. The rule in those days was that if a person could build a house, complete with roof,

Worbarrow. Photo: Crown copyright

in the space of one day, then he was permitted to remain in the area; and this is precisely what the Millers did.

Whereas Henry Miller and his wife Louisa's 'Hill Cottage' was situated at the foot of Gold Down, above the coastguard station, Jack Miller (known as 'Jam') and his wife Alice (known as 'Miggie') lived some way up the hill, on the west side of Worbarrow Bay. Alice's middle name was Rose, so they called their dwelling 'Rose Cottage'. Miggie's mother Granny Rose, was something of a character: her favourite newspaper was the *News of the World*, and she greatly enjoyed a drink now and again. 'Sea Cottage', which stood virtually on the shore line, was the home of Joseph Miller and his family.

It was possible to tell, by the distinctive pattern on his jersey, from which village a Dorset fisherman came. The jerseys of the Worbarrow men (which were hand-knitted by the womenfolk) for example, had one horizontal and two vertical strips of ribbing, with little triangles in the centre representing the waves.

In the summertime a lookout was posted, and as soon as the dark shadow of a mackerel shoal was seen, a fishing boat was dispatched to its seaward side to usher it towards the shore; whereupon the men would rush into the water with their nets. (Whiting and mullet were also plentiful hereabouts).

Jack and Miggy Miller at Rose Cottage. Photo: Helen Taylor

Worbarrow Bay, 1908: hauling in the catch! Photo: Joan Brachi

Harriet and Charlie Miller on their Golden Wedding day.
Photo: Crown copyright

Having been boxed and loaded up into carts, some of the catch would be sold locally, whereas the main bulk of it would be taken to the market at Wareham. The Millers also indulged in crab and lobster fishing: the pots being woven from withies – thin branches of willow which were cultivated specifically for the purpose in a dozen or so 'withy beds' alongside the Gwyle stream. For the visitor, the cost of a fresh, dressed crab was sixpence (6d), and a lobster sandwich 9d.

The secret of the fishermen's success was due to the fact that they used 'line maps': a form of triangulation where, when out at sea, they took bearings from various landmarks such as trees, boulders or buildings, by the aid of which they could return to precisely the same spot (i.e. a place where they had found the fish to be plentiful) at future times.

Henry Miller with lobster pots.
Photo: Joan Brachi

Charlie and Harriet Miller lived at 'Fern Cottage'. Harriet had once been a monitor at Tyneham School, and had sung in the church choir for forty years. In their latter years, the couple supplemented their income by selling chocolates, postcards and sweets to the visitors. They also kept chickens and sold the eggs.

Occasionally, a sailing boat would put in at Worbarrow, and the crew would lodge overnight at one of the fishermen's cottages; otherwise, vessels did not normally encroach on the fishing grounds. A paddle steamer, however, could often be seen sailing between Lulworth and Swanage.

8

THE COASTGUARDS

The coastguard station at Worbarrow (established circa 1865) consisted of the main building (black in colour, having been weather-proofed with tar for protection against the gales), a watch-house with views across the bay, and a boathouse and slipway where the coastguards kept their boat, which also served as a lifeboat.

Another lookout post was situated on the top of Worbarrow Tout, complete with flagstaff and railings. A series of marker stones, painted white, were placed along the pathway to the Tout and the half-mile long cliff path to Kimmeridge Bay, to guide the officer and minimise the

Coastguard Station, Worbarrow. Photo: Joan Brachi

John Weeks, coastguard officer of Worbarrow, with his men.
Photo: Crown copyright

danger of him falling over the cliff when he was on patrol. Two signal cannon: one positioned on top of the Tout and the other adjacent to the main building, were to be fired in case of emergency. Otherwise, the nearest lifeboat station was at Kimmeridge (established by the RNLI in 1868 and closed in 1896).

In the early 1900s, the coastguard station was manned by Chief Officer John Weeks, and six other men. They wore naval-style uniforms, and were equipped with cork lifejackets. Every Friday, Officer Weeks would visit Tyneham School to drill the children in the school yard and supervise them as they exercised with dumb-bells. In fine weather, his men would take residents and visitors on pleasure trips around the bay.

The expense of establishing and maintaining a station here was justified for the following reasons: this was an inhospitable coast where, in a gale, a ship could easily find itself being blown onto a lee shore, which in this case would probably be a rocky cliff; there were also the added hazards of rocky outcrops such as Broad Bench to the east, and the Kimmeridge Ledges which stretched out into the sea like black fingers.

Summer 1898: coastguards taking villagers on trip around the bay. Photo: Crown copyright

It was the habit of the coastguards to row their boat around the coast to the town of Weymouth to re-stock with food and provisions. In March 1865, however, there was a tragedy in which five coastguards from Worbarrow were drowned in a southerly gale on their return journey from that place. On Christmas Day in 1883, the coastguards went to aid the paddle steamer *South of Ireland*, which had grounded on a rocky ledge in thick fog, 200 yards to the east of Worbarrow Tout. Despite the fact that the vessel had broken in two, all her passengers and crew were rescued, with the help of a tug and two barges which arrived on the scene from Weymouth. By a strange coincidence, one of the survivors had formerly been a coastguard at Worbarrow, so he was able to join his former colleagues for their Christmas Dinner. The skipper of the vessel, Captain Pearn, was subsequently found to be negligent and dismissed from the service by the Great Western Railway which owned the shipping company.

In material terms, having the coastguard station at Worbarrow Bay was not in the best interests of the residents of Tyneham and Worbarrow, who in previous times, had undoubtedly benefited materially from the wrecks of the sea. An uneasy relationship also existed between the coastguards and the fishermen. The Millers regarded anything washed up on the shore as fair game, whereas the coastguards believed it their duty to impound it. In particular, the former were dependent on wood washed up on the shore from wrecks for stoking their winter fires.

When the coastguard station closed, Mr Bond decided to remove the paving stones from their site and use them to make a new pavement (complete with kerb) for The Street, which, as Miss Taylor said, 'made a nice finish to the village.' Everyone lent a hand, including Curtis, the Head Gardener at Tyneham House; Tom Gould, the Second Gardener; Fred Curtis, the shepherd's son (who lived at the second cottage in The Row); also two masons who came to work for Mr Bond if he needed any work done 'in the building line'. These were Harry Sturmey, who bicycled in every day from West Knighton (he lived with his mother and therefore preferred to go home every night), and his colleague Walter Trent, who lived at Chaldon (and after a while obtained lodgings with Fred Lucas).

9

POST OFFICE, TELEPHONE, NEWSPAPERS

Tyneham's post office was one of the line of terraced houses known as The Row. The building had originally been a bakery in the days when bread was delivered to the villagers, and to the outlying farms by donkey-cart. However, when the Mores family who ran it moved away, baking ceased and, from then on, bread had to be imported from Hibbs the bakers at Corfe Castle. The bakery then became a general stores, run by a Mrs Pitman. When in 1911, Mrs Pitman retired (having married Worbarrow fisherman Joseph Miller), she was succeeded by Mrs Barnes, and it was then that the former bakery became both general stores and post office. Among the items sold were candles – there being no electricity at Tyneham in those days.

During the time of World War I, a telephone was installed in the kitchen at the rear of Mrs Barnes' post office. (This, apart from one at the coastguard station at Worbarrow Bay, being the only one in the area, including Tyneham House). Although it was for private use only, Mrs Barnes did pass on incoming messages, should any arrive for the villagers. Likewise, if a telegram arrived, she would send her young lady assistant to deliver it to the person concerned. She also sent telegrams: the cost being sixpence for a dozen words, and an extra halfpenny per word thereafter.

In 1929, when the General Post Office announced that they proposed to erect a telephone kiosk in the village, this became a matter of great controversy. Mr WH Bond argued that a red telephone box – which was the standard colour – would be a disgraceful eyesore. He declared, that if a kiosk had to be erected in Tyneham, then it should be built of stone. 'The old squire [i.e. Mr WH Bond] wouldn't have a great, red box disgracing his village', said Helen Taylor. Finally, a compromise was reached, and a concrete kiosk was erected which was painted white!

Mrs Barnes, the Postmistress, with her husband and daughter Phyllis, outside Post Office, 1911. Photo: Helen Taylor

Selby the postman came from Wareham by bicycle each day, and having delivered and collected the mail, stayed in a cottage at Worbarrow and waited for his time to go back in the evening. (In the meantime, he would help out on the farm, or do some fishing in the summer, or go ferreting for rabbits in the winter, to while his moments away).

Later, Selby was succeeded by Postman Barlow who rode a red bicycle. Commencing at Steeple, he visited all the outlying farms, before working his way down the Valley to Tyneham House; then to Tyneham Farm, and finally to the village. (Between Steeple and Tyneham there were eight gates to open; then two more on the way to Tyneham House, and another one at the farm). The postmistress at Tyneham Post Office would then deliver the mail around the village, and to Worbarrow. On Sundays however, Barlow had to go to Worbarrow himself on his bicycle. (In those days there was a small letterbox there; by the fisherman's hut). Latterly, Barlow had a motorcycle and sidecar, which helped enormously because, as he said, with a bicycle it was a difficult task to keep the letters and parcels dry in the gales.

Tyneham's telephone box today.

As for newspapers, in early times *The Western Gazette* was delivered by the baker who came from Stoborough near Corfe Castle. (Mrs Emily Taylor the laundress, however, preferred to have her copy posted to her from the newsagents at Wareham). Later, the newspapers were delivered by motor car from Corfe Castle.

10

THE TAYLOR FAMILY

Helen Taylor was born at Tincleton, and in the first year of her life, 1902, she and her extended family, came to Tyneham. They included her parents William and Emily; her brothers Arthur and Bert; her elder sister Bessie; William and Charlie Meech, her mother's sons by her first marriage. (Emily's first husband had been killed in an accident while taking a horse to be shod at Charminster near Dorchester: a steam traction engine had come along and frightened the horse, which reared up and fell on top of him).

William Taylor. Photo: Helen Taylor

William was working in Dorchester when he saw a job advertised for a woodman to work on the Tyneham Estate. Emily was delighted when he applied, and was duly appointed to the post, as it had always been her dream to live by the sea. When they moved to their new home at Tyneham – 'Laundry Cottage' - they discovered that it was the only dwelling in the village to have running water: others were obliged to use the village pump. The reason for this was that all the laundry for both Tyneham House and the rectory was done here - Emily taking over from the previous laundress. In those early days, before wirelesses were in vogue, the villagers used to put their clocks right by listening out for the hooter, which sounded the beginning and the ending of the working day at the clay works at Furzebrook, 4 miles away to the north.

Every Monday morning, Helen Taylor's step-brother Charlie Meech, did the rounds in his cart – known as 'the putt' - collecting the laundry to be washed in a huge, open, 40-gallon 'copper', situated at the rear of the cottage, and lit by a fire of wooden faggots. Having been washed, the laundry was rinsed in two large wooden troughs, before being passed through the rollers of a mangle, and hung out on the line to dry.

Charlie Meech, 'Odd Man' at Tyneham House. Photo: Helen Taylor

A coke stove was kept burning, around the edge of which was a ledge on which Emily stood the irons to keep them hot when she was doing the ironing. Emily was also skilled in the use of plants and herbs for medicinal purposes, and was therefore much in demand – there being no doctor within several miles. As a restorative, she used nettle and dandelion tea. For burns, the cobwebs of spiders were found to be efficacious. Emily was also one of the first to be informed if someone was expecting a baby, when she would attend the birth in the capacity of midwife. As if these duties were not enough, she was also caretaker for the church and school.

As woodman, Emily's husband William performed a variety of tasks. They included: hurdle-making; collecting faggots for the fires; layering hedges; coppicing hazel – from which spars were made to hold the thatch in place when a dwelling was being re-roofed; logging in Tyneham Great Wood, Rookery Wood, or West Plantation. He was also responsible for stacking the timber to be seasoned, prior to it being used by the carpenter or the boatbuilder Louis Stickland of South Egliston, Kimmeridge. Furniture, milking stools, floor boards, handles for tools, cart wheels and numerous other items were made out of wood in those days. (Louis was also a fisherman, as was his father William, who had been the coxswain of Kimmeridge's first lifeboat the *Mary Heape*).

William Taylor's greatest challenge came in 1911, when the ancient elm tree which stood at the top of The Street was found to be diseased and a danger to passers-by. Every able-bodied man in the village turned out to help saw it down and then cut it up - using long, cross-cut saws each manned by two men - a task which took several days. In its place, an oak tree was planted to commemorate the coronation of King George V, which had taken place the year before. The ceremony ended with the singing of the National Anthem. The villagers were then invited by Mr WH Bond of Tyneham House to drink to the health of the Royal Family, after which he presented packets of tobacco to the men, and packets of tea to the women. The children received sweets and bananas.

William Taylor was responsible for looking after the pheasants on the Tyneham Estate. Sometimes, when a broody hen was required to help hatch their eggs, it was his daughter Helen who was sent off on an errand to find one. It was also Helen's task to fetch Polly the pony, who would pull the trap which would take them to Wareham to the shops. (The family were only able to afford the luxury of a pony and trap on account of them having six breadwinners in the family).

A little bell, attached to Polly's harness, which the locals called a 'rumbler', warned people of their approach in the narrow lanes. The journey involved a steep climb to the top of Grange Hill, after which Polly trotted all the way down to the bottom again. They always stopped at Dickers, the pork butchers in Wareham's West Street, and also at the

Emily Taylor, daughters Helen and Bessie, and pony, 'Polly'. Photo: Helen Taylor

World's Stores, in order to buy Polly a packet of sweets as a reward for her endeavours! When on the return journey they reached the foot of Grange Hill, Polly, who by this time was tiring with the weight, not only of Emily and her two daughters, but also of the shopping, would simply refuse to move, leaving the family no choice but to get out and walk.

Every village household kept a pig, and the Taylors were no exception. When the pig was killed, half the meat was sold and the other half would be salted and kept to feed the family for many weeks to come. The Taylors also had a parrot, given to them by one of their neighbours. It was particularly partial to sunflower seeds, which William Taylor always made sure to plant at the end of his row of runner beans. The idea was that when the large, yellow flowers came out they would attract the bees, which would in turn pollinate the bean flowers to give a bigger crop.

Helen Taylor's two brothers, Arthur and Bert, worked at Tyneham Farm. Her step-brother William Meech, worked as gamekeeper on the

Tyneham Estate. Her other step-brother Charlie Meech, the 'odd-man' at Tyneham House, was so-called because he did all the odd jobs. Charlie was known for his ready smile and infectious laughter. His open, two-wheeled cart ('putt'), was drawn by a single carthorse. The cart was used for general haulage and also for muck-spreading, in addition to transporting laundry!

When World War I (known as The Great War) broke out on 4 August 1914, it brought tragedy to the Taylor household, along with countless others. Helen Taylor was aged 12 at the time, and would remain at school for a further two years. Her sister Bessie had already left, and was now helping her mother with the laundry. Helen's brother Arthur (who spoke fluent Arabic) was killed in Palestine and was buried with headstone on the Mount of Olives near Jerusalem. Her other brother Bert was also killed, as was step-brother William Meech. Ten more men from the Parish of Tyneham-cum-Steeple also lost their lives

World War I: The Army at Worbarrow. Photo: John Ritchie

Sisters Helen and Bessie Taylor at Laundry Cottage.
Photo: Helen Taylor

in the conflict. Helen's father William took the news extremely badly and became very solitary in his habits.

Meanwhile, the schoolchildren – Helen included – busied themselves making clothes for the Belgian refugees who had come to England after their country had been invaded by the Germans. The children also raised money for those soldiers and sailors who had been blinded in the conflict, and brought toys to school to send to, 'the little invalids at The London Hospital'.

In 1916, Helen Taylor (who described the day she was enrolled as a pupil as the happiest one of her life, so far) left school to take up the position of seamstress at Tyneham House. As for her mother Emily, she died in 1917 at the age of 52, worn down by work and sadness. When the war ended on 11 November 1918, the occasion was marked by a simple ceremony at the flagstaff and the singing of the National Anthem.

11
TYNEHAM HOUSE

Built in the 14th Century, Tyneham House originally comprised a great hall with two other rooms on the ground floor, and two more on the first floor. Known as the 'old house', it fell into a state of disrepair and was eventually converted into a bakery and lodgings for the dairyman, with the first floor being used as a store room for fruit and potatoes.

The main part of the house – a three-storey building with elegant gables, library, Oak Hall, and drawing room with bedrooms above, was constructed in Elizabethan times. The date 1583 was carved into the stonework above the porch.

A famous visitor to Tyneham was the English writer Celia Fiennes, who between 1685 and 1703 travelled the country on horseback and

Tyneham House, built in Elizabethan times and home to the Bond family since 1683.
Photo: Mark Bond

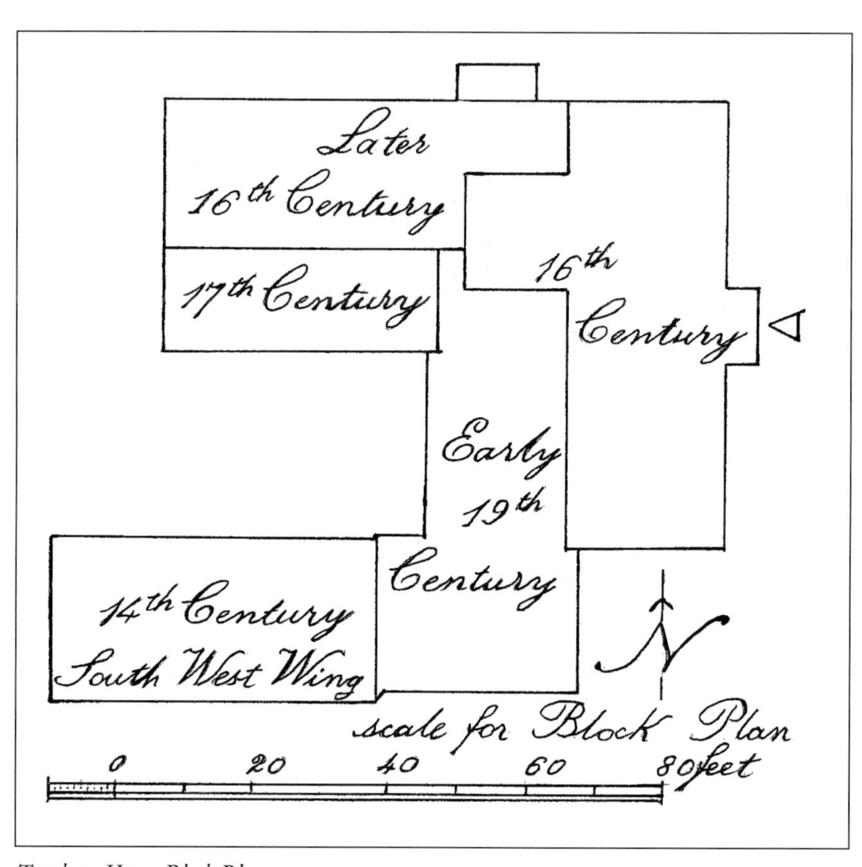

Tyneham House Block Plan

made notes of the places she visited in her travel diary (first published in 1888 and entitled, *Through England on a Side Saddle in the Time of William and Mary*). Of her visit to Tyneham she said:

> At Tinnum Lady Larence's house there is a pretty large house but very old timber built, there I eat the best lobsters and crabs being boyled in the sea water and scarce cold very large and sweet; most of the houses in the island [i.e. the Isle of Purbeck] are built of stone there is so many quarries of stone, this is just by the great cliffs which are a vast height from the sea; here is plenty of provision of all sorts especially of fish.

(This 'Lady Larence' to whom Celia Fiennes referred, was Jane, the wife of Sir Robert Lawrence, who owned the Tyneham Estate in those days).

Early in the 19th Century, the old house and the Elizabethan house were joined together (when a pantry, store room, and dining room were added on the ground floor, with gun room and more store rooms, a school room, and the governess's room above).

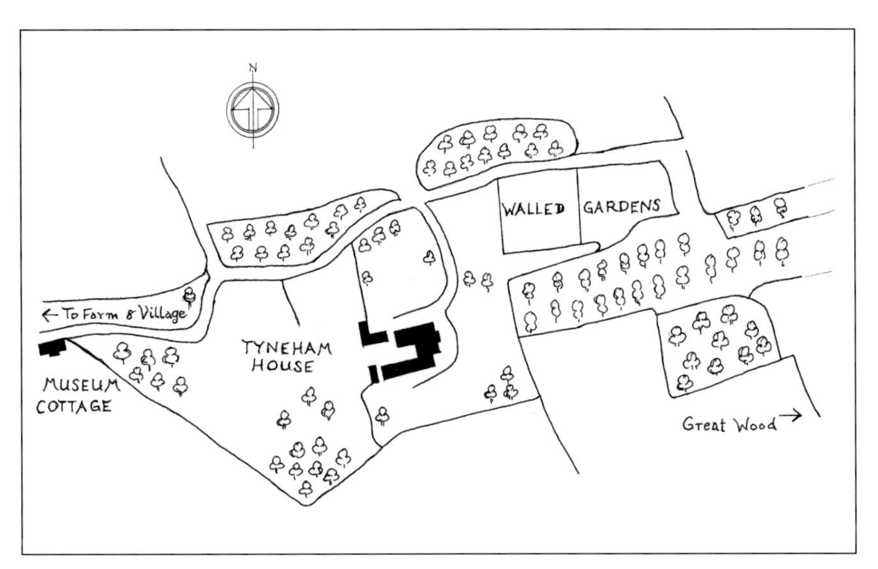

Tyneham House and surrounds

The year 1883 was a special one for two reasons: not only did it mark the 300th Anniversary of the building of the East Wing, but it also marked the 200th Anniversary of its occupancy by the Bond family. In honour of the occasion, all the families on the Tyneham Estate were given a bountiful supply of beef and plum pudding, together with 4 cwt of coal!

The front door of the Elizabethan East Front led into the Oak Hall (the name deriving from the flooring, rather than from the panelling), where the family, traditionally, took tea. To the right was the library, which in more recent times, was the preserve of Mr WH Bond (owner of the Tyneham Estate); to the left was the drawing room – panelled in late Georgian days. Behind that was a dining room facing south, with a passage leading to kitchen, store room and pantry. Upstairs were

The village wall under repair, circa 1900. Left to right, Tom Gould (Under-Gardener and later Head Gardener), Harry Stermey (Mason of Coombe Keynes), Walter Trent (labourer), Fred Lucas (Shepherd's son), Curtis (Head Gardener), Charlie Meech (Odd-man and Carter), and 'Palmer' the horse. Green baize aprons were the gardeners' badges of office. In background the iron guard around the 'Coronation Oak'. Photo: Helen Taylor bedrooms, to which some bathrooms had been added in the early part of the 20th Century. In winter, fires were lit in all the living rooms, with a large stove in the hall. There was no hot water in the bedrooms: this was brought up in the mornings in brass containers for washing and shaving; or in the evenings, for washing before dinner. These were placed on the washstand in each bedroom. Adjacent to the north side of Tyneham House was the brew house, built specifically for the purpose of brewing beer.

Maintaining the gardens at Tyneham House, with their extensive lawns and terraces, and the large, walled garden which provided virtually all the necessary fruit and vegetables for the house, was a major undertaking, as Tom Gould (husband of Virtue), a villager who had served in World War I and survived, could testify. Having commenced as Under-Gardener at Tyneham House, Tom rose to become Head Gardener on the retirement of his predecessor Mr Curtis. However, prior to World War I, Tom had left the village to join the Dorset Regiment, in which he served at Chitral on India's north-west frontier. He then returned to Tyneham and joined up again at the outbreak of hostilities in 1914, serving all through the four long years of war.

His wartime experiences left Tom prone to tremors (the after-effects of shell-blast) and from shortness of breath, due to the poison gas which had entered his lungs. However, slowly but surely, he regained his health and strength, and was able to put in a total of over 40 years service as Gardener at Tyneham House. He never spoke, however, of his wartime experiences in France and Belgium.

12

THE BONDS

The Bond family came originally from Cornwall, and some of its members had achieved fame, not to say infamy, well before they ever set foot in Tyneham! For example, Dennis Bond was one of the commissioners engaged in the trial of King Charles I in the English Civil War; Thomas Bond was comptroller in the household of Queen Henrietta Maria (mother of Charles II), and was instrumental in the building of Bond Street in London; John Bond was a merchant who travelled widely and was not averse to indulging in a little privateering, should the opportunity arise; finally, Lady Alice Lisle (granddaughter of William Bond of Blackmanston in Purbeck) had the misfortune to be sentenced to death by Judge Jeffreys for harbouring a refugee at the time of the Battle of Sedgemoor. This was during the Monmouth Rebellion of 1685. She was beheaded at Winchester on 2 September of that year.

Tyneham had been the country seat of the Bond family since 1683. In the 19th Century, Jane, wife of the then owner the Reverend William Bond, had insisted on having the mullioned windows on the ground floor of the east front enlarged, in order to admit more light. When the Reverend William died in 1852, his eldest living son the Reverend John Bond, was parish priest at Weston near Bath (in which capacity he served for 55 years). Therefore, from this year until John's retirement in 1891, his younger brother Thomas kept house at Tyneham and managed the estate.

Thomas was a barrister at law, an antiquarian, and one of the founders of the Dorset County Museum. He wrote many books and papers including: *A Description of Corfe Castle* (1865); *The Ancient Manor Houses of the Isle of Purbeck* (1867) and *The Families Anciently Residing in the Isle of Purbeck* (1868). He also edited (with the Rev. C Bingham) the Purbeck section of the Reverend John Hutchins' *History and Antiquities of the County of Dorset.*

The Reverend John Bond, despite living in Somerset, maintained a

Thomas Bond (1805 – 1873).
Photo: Mark Bond

The Reverend John Bond (1801-1898).
Photo: Mark Bond

Mr WH Bond and his wife Mary in 1914, on the day of their daughter Lilian's wedding.
Photo: Margot Bond.

lively interest in Tyneham (albeit of a more practical nature), as is evidenced by his account of how the village obtained its water. In 1853, a tap (fed presumably by a spring) and water trough had been erected at the top of The Street, in memory of the Reverend William Bond who had died the year before. In September 1888, the Reverend John wrote:

> The Spring in Madmore [on the lower slopes of Whiteway Hill, to the north of the village] produces:
> 1 pint in 15 seconds
> 30 gals. [gallons] per hour
> 720 gallons in 24 hours.
>
> Thus 12 cottages in Tyneham may have [obtain] from the above spring, 60 gallons, or about 15 buckets a day. When the spring in Madmore was brought down to the village by pipes in 1888, a still larger supply of water was found to issue from a draining pipe just above the upper tank, apparently from a spring arising somewhere near the hedge separating Church Furlong from Madmore, and [this] was conducted into the tank. The quantity of water it produced was not measured, nor has it been ascertained whether it is continuous.

When Helen Taylor arrived at Tyneham with her family in the year 1902, William Henry Bond (or Mr WH Bond as he preferred to be called – rather than 'squire'), born in 1852, was the incumbent at Tyneham. Formerly a lieutenant in the Royal Scots, he had inherited the estate in 1898 on the death of his uncle the Reverend John Bond.

Mr WH Bond enjoyed reading the newspaper, and in his early years at Tyneham, he took *The Western Gazette*. In his later years he took *The Globe*. However, due to the remoteness of the area, this presented a problem, in that the paper did not arrive at Creech (on the north side of the hill) until the afternoon, when it was delivered along with the mail. Therefore, by the time it had been collected, ironed by the butler, and placed on the table in the Oak Hall, the news was a day late!

Sometimes, as a special treat, the village children were invited to a tea party at Tyneham House: held in the garden, weather permitting.

Ginger nuts and sugar plums were on offer, and races were held along the terrace wall. Afterwards, the Bonds gave each child a present, such as a doll for the girls, or a wooden train for the boys.

As far as the Tyneham Estate was concerned, Mr WH Bond was a stickler for tidiness. He could not abide the sight of a thistle, for example, and was often to be seen prowling around with his hoe, ready to perform summary execution on any that he might discover! His habit of walking around with his mouth open, earned him the nickname 'Flycatcher'.

To Mr WH Bond's wife Mary, fell the responsibility of presiding over the large household at Tyneham. This included: cook, head housemaid-cum-lady's maid, under-housemaid, Mrs Bond's personal maid, kitchen maid, scullery maid, butler, parlourman, and footman. Mrs Bond also kept a watchful eye on the health of the villagers, and anyone who fell ill could be sure of a nourishing bowl of soup and a pudding. To fetch the doctor, meant a journey of 4 miles on horseback to the village of Wool, whereupon he would arrive in a dogcart attired in a long frock-coat. This might take several hours; so Mrs Bond always kept a plentiful supply of medicines, bandages and herbs to hand in case of emergency. In her spare time, Mrs Bond sang, and was proficient in both piano, harp and organ.

13

THE BOND CHILDREN

The Bonds had five children: Algernon (Algy) was the eldest, then Ralph, Cicely, Lilian, and Margot, who were looked after by a nurse, Miss Hannah Hurworth from Gainford in County Durham; she had joined the household in 1888. Tall, thin and dignified with grey hair, Miss Hurworth's long skirts made a swishing sound as they brushed along the floor as she walked. So attentive to her duties was she, that Mrs Mary Bond frequently had to order her out into the garden so that she might obtain some fresh air! The problem was finally solved, when Miss Hurworth was given the task of supervising the procurement of fruit from the garden for the table; this meant that she simply could not avoid going outside!

Miss Hurworth was also responsible for sewing and darning, and it was she who taught Helen Taylor to sew when the latter joined the household staff in 1916. Of this, there was always more than enough to do – making clothes for the Bonds' children, making sheets, curtains and

Miss Sokolova with Cicely Bond and 'Amos' the terrier.
Photo: Margot Bond

Algy, Margot, and Ralph Bond, before Algy sailed for the South African War.
Photo: Mark Bond

covers, darning, and even running up an item or two for the children of the village. Louisa Longman of Baltington Farm (known as Louie) for example, was delighted when a little brown suit, which had belonged to Miss Margot Bond, was altered to fit her.

Mr WH Bond and his wife Mary employed Anna Petrovna Sokolova (who was half-German and half-Russian) as the childrens' governess. They promptly nick-named her 'Socky', and she was allocated a first-floor room in Tyneham House. The only other member of staff permitted to reside on this floor was Nurse Hannah Hurworth. Next door was the school room, where the day's lessons commenced at 9 a.m. sharp. Socky was not only a fine linguist, but also a musician, and she was often to be heard going through her repertoire of operatic arias whilst accompanying herself on the piano. Although Socky's room faced south and afforded fine views of the avenue of lime trees which led up to the house, she was forever complaining about the cold, and also about the quality of the cooking. The problem was that, because of Tyneham's remoteness, Mrs Bond found it extremely difficult to keep a cook for any length of time.

Algernon, the eldest son (known as 'Algy'), was educated at Eton (as was his brother Ralph). As a child, he was fascinated by maps and atlases of the world, and longed for adventure. This he found, when he joined the army and went to South Africa as a lieutenant in the Rifle Brigade to fight in the Boer War. Having been severely wounded at the Siege of Ladysmith, he was admitted to the hospital there. Despite the fact that the hospital lay outside the town's perimeter fence, the Boers, to their credit, allowed its work to continue and also permitted it to be re-supplied by the defenders. When Mr WH Bond learned of his son's predicament, he travelled to South Africa himself; he hired an ox cart and two natives, and joined the column of the Commander-in-Chief General Sir Redvers Buller. When, in February 1900 (after almost 4 months) the Siege of Ladysmith was lifted, Mr WH Bond was one of the first to enter the town to be reunited with his son.

Algy having arrived safely back in Tyneham, his parents expressed their thanks for his safe return by having a new pipe organ installed in the church. This replaced the harmonium, which had in turn replaced the barrel organ. Having regained his health and strength, Algy returned, for a time, to South Africa before rejoining the 2nd Rifle Brigade in India. Here, he was to be struck down by another tragedy: whilst on leave, he went on a shooting expedition with a companion named Powell and contracted cerebral malaria, which proved to be fatal. He died in 1911 at the age of thirty-one. Algy's parents subsequently installed a stained-glass window to his memory in Tyneham church.

Having left Eton, Ralph, the Bond's second child went up to New College, Oxford, where he rowed for the University. (His 'Oxford oars' were hung on the north walls of Tyneham House's brew house). He then moved to the Sudan, where he lived for many years, pursuing a career in the Political Service. Meanwhile, his three sisters, Cicely, Lilian and Margot, remained at home to be educated by the governess. The library at Tyneham House included a large collection of books on natural history, described by Lilian as 'an abiding joy', and clearly this was a great stimulus to the children's love of the subject. In fact, when the cottage at the western end of Rookery Wood was vacated by the gardener (who preferred to live in the village), this became known as Museum Cottage because this is where the children would keep their natural history collections. (The cottage was later occupied by the coachman).

Paddle-steamer VICTORIA in Lulworth Cove. Photo: Crown copyright

When paddle steamers began to call in at Worbarrow Bay, those wishing to board the boat did so by means of a wooden trolley on wheels, which was pushed out from the beach into the water. Now it was possible for everybody, including the Bond sisters, to travel to Weymouth for shopping and sightseeing (prior to this it had been necessary to row to Arish Mell, and then to walk to Lulworth Cove and catch the steamer there). High on the cliff top, beside the path leading to Kimmeridge, the Bonds erected a shelter with a large stone bench known as 'ocean seat', where people could sit and watch the boats plying up and down the Channel.

Christmas was a time when the sisters had enormous fun putting on entertainments, which they planned for weeks, or even months ahead. At first, these were held in the schoolroom, but proved so popular that larger premises had to be sought. Farmer Walter Case Smith came to the rescue by offering them the use of his barns, where they built a stage and erected the scenery. People came from miles around to the 'Tyneham Theatre' where the three sisters performed to packed houses of 150 people or more.

Lilian Bond, born 1887, with 'Amos' and 'Daniel', her Aberdeen terriers. Photo: Mark Bond

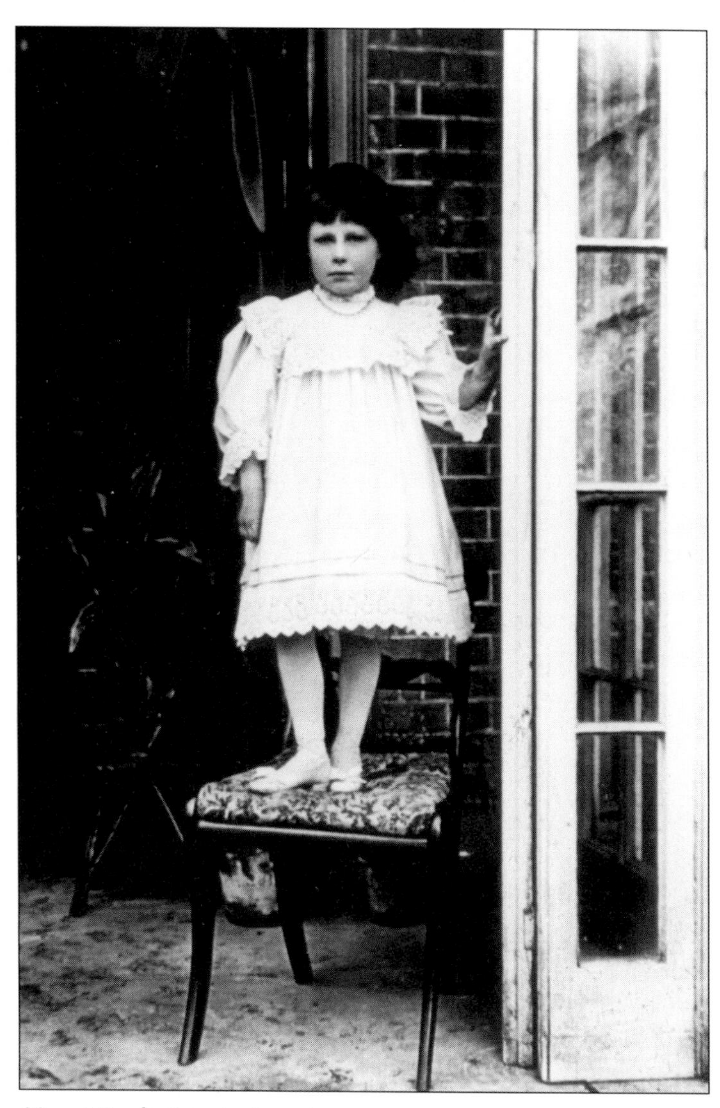

Margot Bond. Photo: Mark Bond

Everyone looked forward to a visit from the mummers – a dozen men who would arrive at Tyneham sometime between Christmas Day and Twelfth Night to perform plays, of which *St George and the Dragon* was the favourite. As well as acting the parts of 'The Turkish Knight', 'The Saracen', 'The fair Sabrina' and of course, 'Father Christmas', the mummers also supplied a fiddler and a serpent player (the serpent being a wind instrument of tubular, convoluted shape). After the performance, when the mummers had been rewarded with their fee, they were plied with beer, brewed in the brew-house by William Woadden, the Bonds' butler. (Ralph, Mr WH Bond's son, declared that this was the finest beer he had ever tasted). All profits went towards the provision of a recreation hut for the village. The sisters also assisted at the village Sunday School.

In 1910, Cicely Bond was married at Tyneham Church to Lewys Legg Yeatman, Barrister, of Hartlebury Castle, Worcester. The couple set up home at Stock Gaylard in North West Dorset. In 1914, also at Tyneham Church, Lilian Bond married Herbert Ivo de Kenton Bond, her namesake of nearby Grange and went to live at Weybridge in Surrey. However, whenever they visited Tyneham, both sisters continued in their tradition of helping at the Sunday School. A diligent correspondent, Lilian wrote a letter home to her mother every day of her married life. In the same year, baths and central heating were installed at Tyneham House. However, the radiators were never particularly effective, despite the fact that the boiler devoured enormous quantities of coke!

Unlike her siblings, Margot Bond, the youngest of the children, did not marry. She continued to live at home, where she played a full part in the life of the village. When, at the end of World War I, some prefabricated huts at Wareham (in which the returning soldiers of Kitchener's army had been billeted) were put up for sale, Miss Margot duly purchased one and had it brought back to Tyneham. Here, it was re-erected in the grounds of the gardener's cottage, where it would now serve as a recreation hut for the village. All that was needed was a piano; once again, Margot was fortunate in that Tyneham School had just been

Hannah Hurworth in the spring of 1912, holding Cicely's son John Yeatman. Photo: Helen Taylor

The Bonds having fun. Photo: Mark Bond

presented with a new one by the Dorset County Council, and was therefore getting rid of its old one (which had been originally purchased with the proceeds from a garden fête held at Tyneham House).

By the 1920s, the occasional car was to be seen in the Valley, and when Margot Bond made her first trip to London in such a vehicle, she reported, with great excitement, that from Wareham onwards and all the way to the capital city, the roads were tarmacadamed.

With the death of the Bonds' butler William Woadden, home-brewing at Tyneham House came to an end. The brew house fell into disrepair, and thereafter beer was brought in from outside. Mr WH Bond now rebuilt and enlarged the brew house, and it became a playroom for the young, complete with table tennis table and huge fireplace. At Christmastime, this is where the tree was placed for the traditional seasonal present-opening ceremony, enjoyed by the whole household as they warmed themselves in front of the fire which burned in the huge fireplace.

14

REGGIE WARE

Another survivor of World War I was Reginald Gower Ware (born in 1891 and known as 'Reggie'), whose association with Dorset dated from his childhood days, when he and his family used to come down from their home in Bath for holidays. They stayed in the Clavell Tower, situated on the cliff-top at Kimmeridge, where Reggie's father Walter Thomas Ware (horticulturalist from Barrow castle, Bath) had designed the custom-built furniture – tables, bookcases etc – for the Tower, making them round in shape, to fit the walls. (Known locally as 'the pepper pot' on account of its shape, the Tower was built between 1830-31 as a folly by the Reverend John Clavell, who had inherited the nearby Smedmore Estate in 1817. Later it was used as a coastguard lookout post).

Reginald Gower Ware on sick leave, circa 1917. Photo: Ione Heath

Having studied engineering at Reading University, Reggie joined the army at the outbreak of World War I in 1914, and was commissioned the following year into the Royal Army Medical Corps. Having been severely wounded by shell splinters whilst serving in the French Zone, he was pronounced unfit for further service and demobilized in 1917.

Reggie Ware's car, parked beside the Clavell Tower. Photo: Ione Heath

Reggie had always been fascinated by motor cars – his older brother Sydney being works manager for the Straker-Squire Motor Company of Bristol. Described as 'an exciting driver', Reggie himself owned a succession of cars which included: a 'Graham Paige Six' (American - produced in 1928, with 23.4 horsepower and a 4-speed gearbox. The car sold in the UK for £475); a Packard (American); an NSU (German); a Mercedes Benz (German), and a Jaguar coupé (British). As a result of his war wounds, his left arm was virtually useless, so the gearboxes of his cars had to be adapted for use by the right arm. (The road to the Clavell Tower was steep, obliging him to drive his car – heavily laden with a large wooden box of provisions – in reverse in order to cope with the gradient).

Reggie had also been wounded in the abdomen and this had an adverse effect on his digestive system, leaving him as thin as the proverbial rake, and obliged to adhere to a special diet. Nevertheless, he enjoyed a cigarette, and continued to smoke throughout his life. Also, he believed that sleeping in damp sheets was efficacious.

With fond memories of childhood holidays at Kimmeridge, Reggie, who already owned a property in Dorset, decided to make nearby Tyneham his home. Here, at Gate Cottage near the lower end of the Gwyle stream (to which incidentally he added a garage to house his car), he could find peace and tranquillity, and also indulge another of his passions – fishing. (His boat was called *Witch of Worbarrow*). Having private means, he had no financial worries. Another attraction of Tyneham – or more particularly Worbarrow – was that here was situated the holiday home of his grandfather John Wheeler, and John's second wife Mary Jane, whose dwelling was known as 'The Bungalow'.

15

THE COACHMAN

Coachman Fred Knight and his family lived at Museum Cottage, situated on the west side of Tyneham House, at the edge of Rookery Wood. (Fred's predecessor Sydney Mills had retired, having almost lost his life when the dog-cart which he was driving overturned in the snow – following which he lost his nerve).

Fred made frequent visits to Wareham, either in the coach when he was transporting visitors, or in the dog-cart when he was collecting provisions. Every quarter of the year he would go to Wareham station to fetch an order, placed by the Bonds with the Army and Navy Stores in London. The journey to Wareham was too much for horses to accomplish

A proud day for coachman Fred Knight and his young groom: Cicely Bond's wedding, 1910.
Photo: Mark Bond

in a single day, so they were rested overnight at the town's Red Lion Inn.

Fred's son Fred junior (who was born at Museum Cottage) later recorded his own memories of Tyneham in his publication *The Rooks in the Elm Trees: a Tyneham Boyhood*:

> I was born to the sound of rooks and with the sea air in my lungs. It was June 8, 1908, and I knew nothing else about the rest of the world, only that I was alive, and with Mother, and that nature was all around me. Through the open window of our bedroom was a leafy paradise, the rooks were cawing high above me, and the cool breeze was blowing up the valley straight off the bay. It was summer, and life was good!

Fred junior remembered queuing with his school friends at the village tap, where they would cup with their hands to get a drink, before returning to play chase, or with their hoops. Also:

> climbing onto the back of Miss Margot Bond's donkey 'Blitz', whereupon the creature promptly put his head between his front legs, started bucking and jumping and I finished up in a bed of stinging nettles.

And, going with one of the Miller fishermen in a boat to Gad Cliff, where he clambered over the jagged rocks to collect seagull eggs which were eaten by the family, and which his mother used for making cakes. Fred's best friend was Billie Mintern (who was drowned in a boating accident at Worbarrow, aged 16). In the 1912 Tyneham School photograph, Billie is seen holding the blackboard, with Fred sitting to his left in the front row, three places along.

Fred described how, if ever he went near his father when he (i.e. the latter) was working, he always found a 'little' job for him to do, which was, invariably, to clean the horses' curb chains:

> These two small hooks, that went under the horse's jaw, were constantly being soiled by its saliva. First, we washed them (the hooks) in a bucket of cold water, then we buried them in a box of dry sand. When we pulled them out, they were caked in this sand, and by rubbing them together, the dirt would dislodge and they began

> to shine. How we rubbed those curb chains. We rubbed and rubbed them until our hands were quite raw!

Fred often accompanied his father to Wareham, where he saw, 'the biggest collection of houses I've ever seen up 'til then.' Said Fred:

> We had no pocket money, not even a few coppers, but then there was nothing much to buy in those days. If you, or anyone else wanted anything, you generally just went without it.

In 1918, when he was aged 10, Fred and his family moved to Povington, from where they could hear guns firing at Portland to mark the end of World War I.

16

THE RETURN OF RALPH BOND

In the Spring of 1920, Ralph, now the Bond's eldest and only son (following the death of Algy in 1911), returned from the Sudan and married Evelyn, daughter of the late Colonel Arthur Blake. For some years, it had been the custom of the Colonel and his family to take Smedmore House near Kimmeridge, seat of the Mansel family, for the summer. The Blakes had five daughters (all three of their sons having also been killed in World War I), and they and the Bonds became firm friends. Ralph and Evelyn's wedding took place at the Blake family's local church at Hinton Admiral in Hampshire.

In 1924, Ralph was appointed Governor of the Dongola Province of the Sudan. Whilst he was in that country, he made a point of rescuing sick and orphaned animals, which he kept in his animal sanctuary at Wad Madani, south of Khartoum on the Blue Nile.

William Ralph Garneys Bond ('Ralph') as bridegroom. Photo: Mark Bond

Finally, in 1926, Ralph returned to Dorset to live at Broadmayne near Dorchester, bringing with him a young female giraffe which he presented to Regent's Park Zoo. She was given the name 'Maudie', and became a favourite with visitors, including his own children Elizabeth and Mark. (The latter followed family tradition by going to Eton). Ralph and his family made frequent visits to Tyneham, usually in the school holidays, where Elizabeth and Mark enjoyed sitting in Odd-man Charlie Meech's cart; each on a wicker basket-ful of laundry, which had been collected from Tyneham House to be taken to Laundry Cottage.

Mr WH Bond died in 1935 at the age of 83, and was buried in Tyneham Churchyard. His widow Mary, and their daughter Margot then moved to Dorchester, and in order to raise the money required to pay death duties, Tyneham House was let to a Dr Hans Sauer. Sauer, born in South Africa in 1857, studied medicine in Britain before returning to South Africa and becoming Medical Officer of Health at Kimberley, where he met Cecil Rhodes. In 1893, Sauer became Managing Director of the Rhodesia Exploration and Development Company Limited, and in the Matabele Rebellion of 1896, he and a handful of men, all unarmed, accompanied Rhodes to the Matopos to make peace with the leaders of the insurgency. Although Dr Sauer's lease was for a two-year period, he vacated Tyneham House before his tenancy agreement had expired. This followed a tragic accident in which his nephew was killed, falling from his horse onto a stone gatepost whilst riding at Baltington.

Finally, in 1938, Ralph and his family returned to Tyneham. A number of improvements were now made to Tyneham House, including the installation of electric lighting, and a telephone, the number of which was Kimmeridge 223. In those days, the mail would always arrive in time for breakfast, with a second post in the afternoon. (Mail was delivered and collected daily, even on Sundays).

An expert naturalist, Ralph now became an enthusiastic member of the Dorset Natural History and Archaeological Society, and enjoyed organizing field trips in the vicinity of Tyneham. When the Great Wood, which was ravaged by the gale of 1929 with the destruction of many of its sycamore trees began to recover, he was greatly relieved that it was once again able to provide a roosting place for owls. He once gave a lecture on bats to the Nature Reserve Investigation Committee – a body which proposed that the State should take much greater responsibility for the conservation of plants and wildlife.

17

SHEEPLEAZE

In 1911 a large house named 'Sheepleaze' – enormous by Tyneham standards – appeared on the cliffs to the west of Worbarrow Tout, on lands owned by the Bonds of Grange. This was to the great annoyance of the Bonds of Tyneham, who were loath to permit any new building to take place on their estate.

Warwick Draper was a barrister with a busy practice in London, and he had built 'Sheepleaze' as a summer holiday retreat for himself, his wife Grace, and their three children Philip, Mary and Christopher (known as 'Christo'). In the grounds was a long, thatched building, designed by the Drapers to accommodate their visitors, who included stage and

'Sheepleaze', Worbarrow, built 1910. Photo: Meg Kingston

Mary Pickford (seated, left) and friends at Worbarrow Bay, September 1921. Photo: Joan Brachi

Christo Draper's father Warwick, taking him and his elder brother Philip for a ride. Photo: Meg Kingston

No 1. LOADING UP AT THE STATION –
"Plenty of room yet!"

No. 2. ON THE TOP OF GRANGE HILL –
"Oh dear! That must be the Church Tower at Steple!"

screen personalities from their London social circle. On one holiday, for example, they were joined at Worbarrow by the American film star Mary Pickford.

In wintertime Grace Draper bought in firewood for the fishermen who, in return, kept her well supplied with fish. As for the children, they were given little chores to do: Christo, for example, was regularly sent on an errand to fetch eggs for the household from Harriet Miller (wife of Charlie the fisherman) who kept chickens. In fact, whenever the Drapers visited from London, it was Charlie who transported them to and from Wareham railway station with his horse and wagon.

On the occasions when Christo's father Warwick, was unable to join them for their holidays at 'Sheepleaze' owing to pressure of work, Christo would write him letters, giving an account of his and the family's activities, complete with illustrations, made by him in his own unique and imaginative way. In them he describes: fishing trips; 'blue-belling' and 'primrosing'; seeing an owl fly out from a rabbit hole; having a picnic at Brandy Bay; going 'birds nesting [i.e. collecting eggs] in the goyle'.

Christo's delightful drawings illustrate such events as the Drapers' possessions being loaded from the London train onto the wagon at Wareham, and the journey back over Grange Hill. Finally, when they reach home – 'Sheepleaze' – a small boy, presumably Christo, is depicted standing on top of the wagon throwing off the box labelled 'EGGS WITH CARE' and saying, 'Catch, Beat!' (Beat being presumably the abbreviated nickname of Helen Taylor, also known as 'Beattie'). Meanwhile, Charlie Miller's wife Harriet, holding a bottle in one hand, and what appears to be a pet pig in the other, can only watch in consternation. (In the main, Christo made his own drawings, but occasionally, these were done by his father and the boy simply coloured them in).

18
SMUGGLING

Like all small boys, Christo Draper was fascinated by tales of the smugglers, and in *A Smuggling Story* he describes how:

> Once upon a time long ago a sailing ship with smugglers on board came sailing round from Swanage, way past St Aldhelm's Head, and landed in Brandy Bay. Their cargo was kegs of brandy. They rolled and hauled them over the rocks until they came to the cave.

However, having found that there were more kegs than the cave could contain:

> They had to take the rest of them out in a dinghy. They then tied them together and fastened stones on here and there, then dropped them into the water and the stones made them sink.

Christo also provides a map of the coastline, including the smugglers' cave; a diagram of the dinghy and the kegs strung out along the sea bottom; the depiction of smugglers' weapons, the cave, and the 'centipede' – a tool used by the smugglers to raise and lower the kegs.

Christo, in his smuggling story, was nearer to the truth than perhaps he realized, as Helen Taylor would testify. She once overheard a conversation between Henry Miller and Mr WH Bond concerning the smuggling that used to go on at Brandy Bay, which lies at the foot of the 400-foot high Gad Cliff. Here, the beach could only be reached at low tide by a special pathway created for the purpose. It was, therefore, an ideal place to bring in a lugger from France, in order to land contraband kegs of brandy. These were then stored in a cliff-side cave until the time was right to move them into another cave in the depths of Tyneham Wood - one which was well concealed by being overgrown with brambles or *brimbles*, as the locals called them.

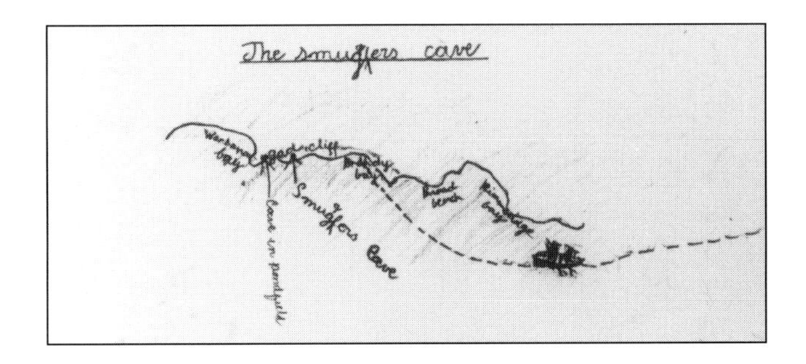
The smuggers cave
Smuggers cave

One of the smu gglers
Then they went on shore again to hunt

Using the centipod for geting kegs out of water.
Centipede used by the smuggers
the smuggers wepons

Miss Taylor saw smuggling taking place before her very eyes when one day, on the seashore at Worbarrow a man came into view riding a big, white horse. She guessed at once that he was a 'surveying man' (one who worked for Customs and Excise). The stranger paused, looked about him, muttered disappointedly to himself, 'There's nothing here', and then proceeded on his way. When he had departed, Helen saw the elderly mother of one of the fishermen rise from the bench upon which she had been sitting to reveal, beneath her long, voluminous skirts, two wooden kegs which she (Helen) assumed to contain smuggled brandy!

At one time, smuggling was so rife along this coast that the Miller fishermen were drafted in as 'extrymen' to assist the coastguards in stamping it out. The Millers for their part, regarded this as a huge joke, for, unbeknown to the coastguards, they were all part of it! As the smuggling went on under the very noses of the Bonds, it is inconceivable that they were ignorant of it. In fact, they almost certainly benefited from it, which brings to mind the lines of Rudyard Kipling's *A Smuggler's Song*: 'Brandy for the parson, 'baccy for the clerk' (or in this case, the squire!).

19

THE BUNGALOW

In the early 1920s another new building, known as 'The Bungalow', appeared on the cliffs above Worbarrow Bay. It was owned by Mrs Mary Jane Wheeler, a widow, whose late husband John was a cotton magnate from the Midlands of England and she herself a descendant of the prison reformer Elizabeth Fry.

The Wheelers had no children of their own, but when both Mary's sister Elizabeth and her husband died, Mary adopted the couple's four children. Over the years, in order to accommodate the extended family, 'The Bungalow' was added to, until finally it contained eight bedrooms and a billiard room with a full-size table. Its window panes had to be of plate glass and one quarter inch thick to withstand the gales! Electricity

The Bungalow. Photo: Joan Brachi

was provided by a 32-volt petrol-driven generator.

Mary Wheeler was often to be seen sitting out in her garden in a wicker chair and sewing, or doing her embroidery. She was a kind and caring person who, at Christmastime, gave parties for the children of the village; always making sure to provide them with a goodly supply of sweets and chocolates which were home-made (using special moulds) by Flo Davis her parlourmaid. Mary also took a special interest in the health and well-being of her late husband's grandson by his first marriage, Reggie Ware, the ex-soldier wounded in World War I - regularly taking him food parcels and bowls of nourishing soup.

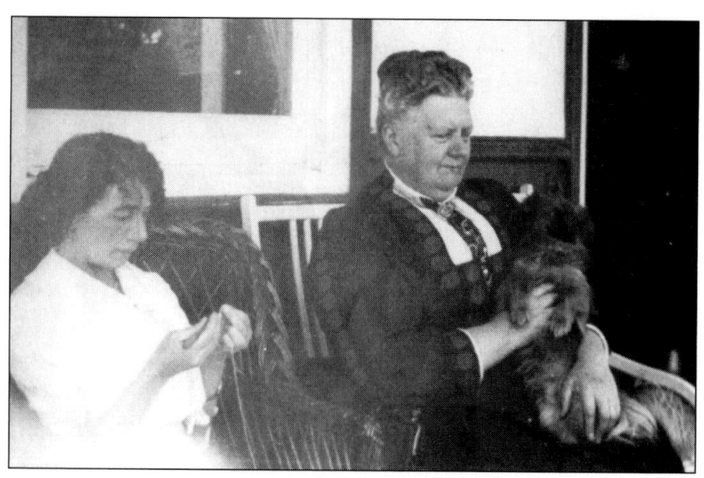

Companion and Mary Wheeler. Photo: Joan Brachi

20

A TYNEHAM ROMANCE

One day, in 1926, a youth named Joe Dando knocked at the side door of Tyneham House. Joe, a stranger to Dorset, hailed from Radstock in Somerset, where his father and five uncles worked in the coal mines. There, the local rector, an enlightened man, was anxious that where possible, the boys of the village be offered an alternative to following in their fathers' footsteps and pursuing the onerous and dangerous career of the collier. To this end, he placed an advertisement in *The Western Gazette* recommending boys for 'gentlemens' service. Mrs Mary Bond of Tyneham House saw the advertisement, answered it, and now here was Joe (who had travelled by train to Wareham and from there by bus to Corfe Castle, then walked the rest of the way), suitably scrubbed, polished, and ready to present himself for interview. The knock at the door was answered by the parlourmaid Alice Rose Wellman – known as 'Rose', the granddaughter of Shepherd Lucas, whose parents lived in a semi-detached cottage situated in the woods below Laundry Cottage. Rose's father Bob worked at the army camp at Lulworth, while her mother Elizabeth brought up their six children, and also found time to help the Taylors with the laundry.

Mrs Bond evidently liked what she saw, because she appointed Joe pantry boy and issued him with a pair of white overalls and a cap. His day began at 7 a.m., when he would prepare the breakfast. In the afternoon he took letters to the post office for posting and collected the milk from Tyneham Farm. Then, whilst Joe was having his afternoon break, Rose, who was the same age as he, made the tea, which was always taken by the family in the Oak Hall. Rose's uniform comprised a white blouse, black skirt, white apron, and a petite, half-round cap worn across her forehead. Dinner had usually been completed by about 9 p.m. after which Joe was free. In those days, there was only Mr WH Bond, his wife

Mary, and their daughter Margot to cater for, except of course when other members of the family or guests came to stay. Joe's Somerset accent was a source of great amusement to the household, and it was some time before either party could fully comprehend what the other was saying!

It was during Joe Dando's time at Tyneham House that a coke boiler and radiators were installed. Until then, each room had been heated by an open fire. Sadly, the boiler proved to be hopelessly inefficient, gobbling up vast quantities of coke. There was no hot water on the upper floors of the house: this was brought up in brass cans in the morning for shaving, and in the evening for washing before dinner. Neither was there any electricity: instead, there were thirty paraffin lamps to be lit and maintained.

On Christmas Day, as Joe, Rose, and the other servants sat down to breakfast together, they found presents from the Bond family on their plates. Joe's was usually a pair of socks! The cook's favourite tipple was 'botanic beer', which she made herself using crystals. When the pheasants were in season, there were shooting parties, the villagers and fishermen combining to act as beaters; after which steak puddings were served in the brew house, where in winter, a great fire burnt.

One day, when Joe was cycling to Wareham to have his hair cut at the barber's shop, he happened to notice great plumes of smoke rising in the distance, from the direction of Lulworth. When he arrived in Wareham, the barber said to him, 'I suppose you have heard about Lulworth Castle? It caught fire in the night.' The castle was the seat of the Weld family, and the year was 1929. In fact, so severe was the fire, that the building was reduced to a shell. All was not lost, however, because by a piece of wonderful good fortune, the two great treasures of the castle, the *Luttrell Psalter* and the *Bedford Book of Hours* had previously been deposited in the British Museum.

For Joe and Rose the course of true love did not run smoothly. Joe was told by Mrs Bond that, there being nothing more that they could teach him at Tyneham, he would therefore have to leave in order to advance himself in his work. By this time, he had served the Bond family for three years. He was broken-hearted, as was Rose. Joe obtained a position first at Blandford, and later at Fritham in the New Forest. Meanwhile, Rose found herself a position at Lyndhurst (also in the New Forest) to be nearer to Joe. When Joe's employer Mrs Holroyd invited Rose to come and be her housemaid, Joe and Rose were reunited, and in 1934 they married. Later, having worked for a time for the Bonds' daughter Mrs Cicely Yeatman in North West Dorset, Joe and Rose finally returned to work at the Manor House at Steeple: she as housemaid, and he as chef. Finally, Joe transferred to an outdoor job at Steeple Leaze Farm, from where he could look down the valley towards Tyneham, and the house where he and Rose had first met.

21

LATTER DAYS OF THE SCHOOL

Winnie Bright lived at Kimmeridge where her father, formerly in the Royal Navy, was a coastguard officer. Her arrival created quite a sensation for the following reasons.

Her appointment as Assistant Teacher at Tyneham School necessitated an arduous walk of 2 miles to work, with the possible added hazard of her boots becoming stuck in the mud, churned up by Farmer Smith's cows, or of being accosted by his gaggle of aggressive and ill-tempered geese which patrolled The Street! However, the solution was at hand! Winnie's father took pity and purchased for her (from Mr Blake's garage

Tyneham School, 1928. Winnie Bright (left), Mrs N Pritchard, Principal Teacher (right) with husband and adopted son Arthur (second from right).
Photo: Crown copyright

at Corfe Castle), a brand new red and black Raleigh motorcycle. She was now able to ride to and fro each day, up and down the valley road, much to the admiration of the pupils – especially the boys!

Winnie was musical by nature, played the piano and gave singing lessons. Her repertoire of military marches was much enjoyed by all. Sadly however, her time at the school was all too short, for having passed the Dorset Education Authority's examination, she was appointed to a teaching post in Swanage, where she met and married a coastguard colleague of her father's!

There was great sadness when in 1932, Tyneham School was forced to close. In its heyday (which was prior to 1912, when the coastguard station had been operational) the number of pupils had risen to a record sixty-eight. Since then, there had been a gradual decline. Following the closure, the children were now either conveyed to school by Mr Sheasby in his taxi, or were obliged to walk to Lulworth to school, depending on which was more convenient. (Mr Sheasby's original 'taxi' had been a horse and cart, which he used to ferry passengers to and from the railway station at Corfe Castle).

22

LEISURE

The village recreation hut, provided by Margot Bond, proved a great success. Here, the children of the village played whist, or watched silent films with the rector Mr Corfield taking charge of the projector (which was operated by the turning of a handle). Louie, daughter of Albert and Emma Longman of Baltington Farm, provided the piano accompaniment. There were also fancy dress parties where Helen Taylor, seamstress at Tyneham House, was usually the one who made the tea. On one occasion, Mabel Cake of West Creech Farm, and her friend Elsie Taylor of Rookery Farm, West Creech, went as 'Nippie' and 'Bob', characters who appeared on posters advertising for Lyon's Corner House. They won First Prize: a set of china jugs which were presented to them by Mr WH Bond. Jumble sales were also held, from time to time, at the recreation hut. A favourite summertime occupation for Mabel Cake was to

With the hay cart at Longman's Farm, Baltington.
Photo: John Ritchie

visit Worbarrow with her younger sister Violet, and, on the way back, call at Longman's Farm, where Mrs Longman would give them tea and 'dripping cakes'.

The great gale of December 1929, not only destroyed many trees in Rookery Wood, West Plantation, and Great Wood but, to everybody's horror, wrecked the recreation hut which was lifted into the air, then dashed to pieces on the ground. Margot Bond (or 'Miss Margot') as she was known to the children, was not to be defeated. At the Ideal Home Exhibition in London, she purchased a brand new hut for the sum of £120, complete with chairs, crockery, and oil stoves with which to heat it. However, she insisted that it be placed in a safer, and less exposed spot – in the woods near to Museum Cottage.

Sylvia House lived with her parents and five siblings at Serley's Living Cottage, Povington Farm, on the north side of the hill. One winter, when snow lay on the ground, Sylvia's father made a wooden sleigh, which they dragged to the top of one of the ancient Iron Age burial mounds; taking turns to sit on it and speed off down the hill. Sylvia recorded how, on her birthday, her mother Jessica had taken her to Wareham. This involved walking across country to a public house called 'The Ragged Cat' on the East Lulworth Road, from where they caught the motor coach into town. Here, her mother bought her the present of a little sewing box.

Arthur Grant's family had moved to Tyneham from Galton near Dorchester in 1924; his father succeeding Helen Taylor's father William, as Tyneham's estate woodman. Their semi-detached cottage (adjacent to that of the Wellman family) had no electricity or running water, and a bucket placed outside the back door served as the toilet (which was the norm in Tyneham village).

Arthur Grant aged 6 years at Tyneham School. Photo: Arthur Grant

As more and more people came to own motor vehicles, so they became more adventurous, and Worbarrow Bay became a favourite place to visit. Young Arthur discovered that a good way of supplementing his pocket money was to volunteer to open and close the gates for the visitors, who obligingly threw him and his fellow entrepreneurs a penny or two from their cars as they sped by. On a good day, a boy might take home as much as three or four shillings. This money would come in useful when the pupils of Tyneham Sunday School had their annual outing to Weymouth and Bournemouth.

A frequent visitor to the area was TE Lawrence – the famous 'Lawrence of Arabia' – on his 'Brough Superior' motorcycle (of which he owned a number during his lifetime). Lawrence showed his impatience when he discovered that the gates (of which, for example, there were no less than seventeen between Worbarrow Bay and Wareham railway station) were closed, and in the absence of youngsters like Arthur Grant to open them, he would charge, head on, on his motorcycle and burst them open! He was therefore, unpopular with the farmers, who one day decided to teach him a lesson by locking them!

Arthur Grant's duty on Sundays at Morning Service, was to work the handle of the pump on the church's barrel organ, as Miss Bowdidge of Grange played hymns. For this, he was rewarded with a sixpence. When Arthur left school he joined the Merchant Navy, and on one occasion, having returned to Tyneham from Africa, he brought back with him a chameleon, which he presented to the Bond children, Mark and Elizabeth, who were fascinated by its ability to change colour. From now on, it lived in the geranium pots which stood in tubs at the west front of Tyneham House. Sadly however, its camouflage proved its downfall, when having strayed onto the lawn, it was run over by the lawn mower (a manual contraption operated by two gardeners: one of whom pushed, while the other pulled).

23
LATER YEARS

Louie (Louisa Winifred Mary), daughter of Albert and Emma Longman of Baltington Farm, grew up and married Stan Sheasby, who was a partner in his family's taxi firm at Corfe Castle. The marriage took place on 18 July 1933, not at Tyneham Church, but at the East Lulworth Chapel: this, because Stan was a Roman Catholic.

A telegram sent from Tyneham Post Office, from all at Baltington Cottage, wished Mr and Mrs Sheasby, the newlyweds, 'long life, health and happiness'.

Miss Hannah Hurworth, the childrens' nurse, died on 11 October 1933 at the age of 86, having served the Bond family faithfully for 45 years. In later years the Taylors, and also the Miller families at Worbarrow, offered accommodation to visitors who came to Tyneham.

Louie and Stan on their wedding day. Photo: Bridget Dixon

The Telegram. Photo: Bridget Dixon

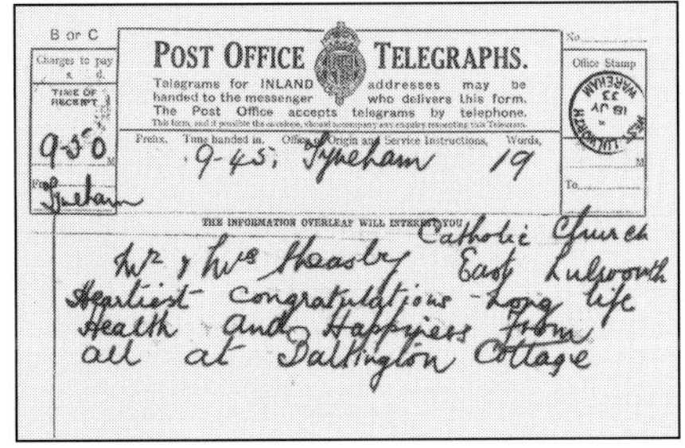

B or C

Charges to pay s. d.

TIME OF RECEIPT 9-50

From Tyneham

POST OFFICE TELEGRAPHS.

Telegrams for INLAND addresses may be handed to the messenger who delivers this form. The Post Office accepts telegrams by telephone.

Prefix. Time handed in. Office of Origin and Service Instructions. Words.

9-45 Tyneham 19

No.

Office Stamp

To

THE INFORMATION OVERLEAF WILL INTEREST YOU

Mr & Mrs Sheasby Catholic Church East Lulworth

Heartiest congratulations long life Health and Happiness from all at Baltington Cottage

Meg Ritchie in her Tyneham wonderland.
Photos: Meg Kingston

The first tractors arrived in Tyneham Valley in 1937: Fordsons, manufactured in America, and each costing £125. Instead of rubber tyres, the wheels were fitted with metal spade lugs which provided traction, but had the disadvantage in wet weather of causing the vehicle to become bogged down, by digging itself into the ground.

Not surprisingly, Christopher Draper – 'Christo' – of 'Sheepleaze', with his artistic ability, grew up to become the author of a number of children's books. He also spent time in Africa, living with the Zulus! His elder brother Philip joined the Shell Oil Company. His sister Mary, married electrical engineer James Ritchie, and the couple set up home at Chiswick Mall, West London. However, the family continued to visit 'Sheepleaze', where they and their children, including daughter Meg, spent many happy holidays.

24
WAR

Even before war broke out on 3 September 1939, the area of Tyneham was already fortified with barbed wire and tank obstacles placed along the beach at Worbarrow. Mines were laid, and occasionally a sheep would tread on one and it would go off.

Ralph Bond of Tyneham House, who whilst at Eton had served in the Officer Training Corps, now created the Tyneham, Kimmeridge, and Steeple platoon of the Home Guard, with himself in command. Meanwhile, Ralph's wife Evelyn joined the Women's Voluntary Service and ran a mobile canteen serving the isolated anti-aircraft batteries, which were set up at strategic places in the countryside.

Following the outbreak of war, the tank gunnery ranges at Lulworth were expanded, and approximately half the entire area of Purbeck was taken over by the army. After Dunkirk, more troops came to Tyneham. Tyneham House was now requisitioned by the Royal Air Force, which had established a radar station on the cliffs at Tyneham Cap above Brandy Bay. This was to accommodate members of the Women's Auxiliary Air Force who were employed at the station. As for their airmen colleagues, they were billeted at the rectory. Having been made homeless, Ralph Bond, his wife Evelyn, and his mother Mary (Mr WH Bond's widow) asked the Taylors if they could come and live with them at Laundry Cottage, prior to them being re-housed at Museum Cottage.

On 11 July 1940, an enemy Messerschmitt Bf110 fighter aircraft was intercepted by Spitfires from RAF Warmwell aerodrome near Dorchester; shot down, and crash landed on Povington Heath. Its two-man crew became the first Germans to be taken prisoner in the Battle of Britain. (Prisoners of war were usually put to work; for example, three Germans were delivered daily to Povington Farm in an army truck to help Farmer Smith). The following month (August 1940), Mark Bond

Ralph Bond, his daughter Elizabeth, wife Evelyn and son Mark in 1941 at Tyneham House. Photo: Mark Bond left Eton and returned to Tyneham for a few weeks, where he served in his father's Home Guard platoon. In September, he enlisted in the Rifle Brigade and was commissioned the following year.

In November 1942, Ralph Bond learned that his son Mark, had been wounded in the Battle of El Alamein. On 17 November 1943, Postman Barlow, who by now had graduated from a bicycle to a motorcycle and sidecar, delivered two letters to Ralph Bond. The first informed him that the army proposed to take over the entire Tyneham Valley, and that everybody was to be evacuated within twenty-eight days; the second that his son Mark was 'missing in action' in Italy. (In fact Mark Bond would survive the war and continue to serve in the army until 1972).

25

TYNEHAM IS EVACUATED

The area to be evacuated included not only Tyneham itself (along with Worbarrow and Baltington), but also Povington and West Creech to the north, North and South Egliston, and Lutton to the east, and East Lulworth to the west.

This was a predominantly farming area, and the following farms were affected: Tyneham, Lutton, Baltington, North Egliston. At West Creech: West Creech Farm, White Hall, Rookery and Hurst Mill. At Povington: Povington Farm, Searleys, Jiggiting Corner and Broadmoor. At East Lulworth: Weld Arms Farm, The Cat, and Whiteway. As far as their livestock was concerned, as many as 313 dairy cows and bulls, nine working horses, seventy-one sheep, thirty-three pigs, and 167 poultry were auctioned by Henry Duke and Son of Dorchester: this was from the Tyneham Valley alone. (The Cat public house at East Lulworth was taken over, but the hamlet of Steeple, together with Steeple Leaze and Blackmanston Farms, escaped the army occupation). Jack and Tom Miller, who were in their sixties, continued fishing right up until the time of the evacuation. By then, Charlie Miller had already retired.

The evacuation of the greater part of the Parish of Tyneham-cum-Steeple, in the December of 1943, was a nightmare for its inhabitants – and in more ways than one. This was a time of year when normally, everyone would have been looking forward to Christmas. Now, in what was a particularly cold winter, a community, which had existed for untold generations, was to be scattered throughout the county of Dorset; to be relocated in such places as Corfe Castle, Langton Matravers, Wareham, and even as far away as Upwey near Weymouth. The inhabitants were therefore denied that emotional support which they could have given to one another at this time of crisis. This was a particularly poignant time for young William Wrixon (known as 'little Billy') of Povington Farm, who was due to celebrate his twenty-first birthday on 15 December.

There were some small consolations however. For example, the Taylor sisters and their father William (whose former home, Laundry Cottage, was now being used as a headquarters for army officers) were relocated to Corfe Castle. Here, for the first time in their lives, they had indoor sanitation and electricity. As for the Bonds of Tyneham House, they also found temporary accommodation at Corfe Castle.

With the ending of the war on 8 May 1945, the inhabitants of Tyneham-cum-Steeple waited anxiously for permission to be given by the government for them to return to their homes. (They had since learned that the gunnery wing of the Royal Armoured Corps Fighting Vehicles Unit at Lulworth had trained the British and American tank crews for the assault on the Normandy beaches). However, that invitation from the government was one which would never come. The call of the villagers was never answered.

26

AFTERMATH

Following the army's occupation of Tyneham, Lilian Bond, despite the fact that she had written extensively about Tyneham in her book, *Tyneham: A Lost Heritage*, refused to return to the Valley, preferring to remember the place as it was.

It is a popular misconception that the Army was in some way to blame for the occupation of Tyneham in 1943. The decision was, in fact, a governmental one based on the perceived requirements of national security. The decision that the army should continue to occupy the larger portion of the Parish of Tyneham-cum-Steeple after the war was again a political one: the War Department having decided that the area was to become permanently incorporated into Lulworth's 7,200 acre tank and gunnery range.

The Army has always treated the village of Tyneham, which lies on the periphery of the ranges (and is therefore not subject to gunfire from the tanks) with respect and reverence. However, as the cottages deteriorated, a certain amount of shoring up work had to be done, to the extent that the first floors and roofs had to be removed for reasons of public safety. As for the cottages at Worbarrow, little now remains. Tyneham School, however, remains intact and is now open to visitors.

As for the church, although it was declared redundant and deconsecrated, the Army arranged for the nave to be re-roofed with tiles (its original lead covering having been stolen after the evacuation). Volunteers, supervised by Roy Cobb, formerly a stonemason and quarryman of Langton Matravers, restored the churchyard and its tombstones and crosses. The church's Jacobean pulpit now resides in the chapel at Lulworth Camp. Of the church's two bells: one is stored at Steeple and the other hangs in the belfry of West Parley church near Bournemouth.

Although Tyneham Church still has most of its original windows, the East window is comparatively new. Designed by Martin Travers as a memorial to Mrs Grace Draper of 'Sheepleaze', it depicts the Madonna and Baby Jesus beneath the umbrella of a gnarled and weeping tree, with butterflies at either side, and one of them (a Camberwell beauty) resting in a fold of Mary's robes. Smaller panes depict the life of Tyneham parish: fishermen putting to sea in their boats; labourers toiling in the fields. The rectory was destroyed in a fire in 1966 and is now an empty shell.

As for Tyneham House, this too became a ruin, the main section, including its east frontage, being demolished in 1968. The loss of any part of our national heritage is to be regretted; the author Evelyn Waugh (in the preface to his novel *Brideshead Revisited*, published in 1945) described 'ancestral seats' (such as Tyneham House) as 'our chief national artistic achievement....'

Ralph Bond, who died in 1952, and his wife Evelyn, who died two years later, were buried at Owermoigne near Dorchester. Also in 1952, William Taylor died at the age of 87 and was buried at the cemetery at Corfe in the lea of the ruined castle. Reggie Ware, who had continued to live in the Purbeck area, died in 1973 at the age of 82. Helen Taylor died in 1998 at the age of 97: she was laid to rest at Tyneham, beside her mother Emily, elder sister Bessie, and her step-brother Charlie Meech – the odd-man.

In 1974, the government made the sum of £10,000 available to be used to create safe footpaths and a car park, in order to give the public greater access to the Tyneham Valley (when the Army was not using it for gunnery practice).

EPILOGUE

For someone such as myself who has heard, at first hand, the story of Tyneham from the people who actually lived there, the sacrifices the villagers were required to make becomes even more poignant. Yet, as an author, I feel remarkably privileged to have been allowed, by them, to share their precious memories of the place they loved so well.

When I first visited Tyneham and surveyed its ruined cottages, farm and rectory (the ruins of Tyneham House being inaccessible as it lies within the gunnery range), I must confess to feeling somewhat downcast, though I was relieved to see that the church and school, at least, had been preserved. Now, when I visit Tyneham I close my eyes and imagine that I can hear the bells of Shepherd Lucas's sheep echoing down the valley; the jingle of the 'rumbler' bell which signalled the approach of the Taylors' pony Polly; the distinctive ting-a-ling of Postman Selby's bicycle bell; most of all, of course, the sound of the church bells ringing out at Christmas, New Year and Easter; or for a village wedding!

I can hear twigs cracking under the boots of William Taylor, as he goes about his work as estate woodman, crushed and desolate after the loss of his two sons in World War I; I can see the downcast face of Mr WH Bond, who helped to rescue his eldest son Algy in 1900 in the Boer War, only to learn of Algy's death from disease in India in 1911.

I hear the sound of the fish trader, standing on the grassy mound known as 'The Knap', calling 'Mac-a-low! Mac-a-low!' at the top of his voice to indicate that he has mackerel for sale. Whereupon, the village housewives would rush out with their plates and purses to purchase half a dozen mackerel for their families' supper. I hear the swish of children's nurse Hannah Hurworth's long skirts, as she takes her long promenade in the grounds of Tyneham House, allowing her eyes to focus on the distant trees, as a welcome change from peering at her needle and thread.

Tyneham Church: the Grace Draper memorial window.

I see in my mind's eye, Helen Taylor mingling with older pupils, as she tries to gain admittance to the school before her time; so thirsty is she for knowledge! Helen's lively intelligence, combined with dignity and devotion, were qualities which those who knew her would never forget. Although naturally sad at the loss of her community at Tyneham, she and her family, as much as any (bearing in mind the loss of family members which had befallen them in World War I), understood that war involves sacrifice. To her credit she accepted her fate with good grace, never displaying any resentment. Nevertheless, Helen always spoke of Tyneham as her home.

I can visualize the young Mark and Elizabeth Bond, perched up on top of wicker laundrybaskets like a little prince and princess, being promenaded around the village by Charlie Meech the odd-man, in his cart. And in my mind's eye, the village comes to life once more!

BIBLIOGRAPHY

Bond, Lilian. 1956. *Tyneham: A Lost Heritage.*
Wimborne: The Dovecote Press.

Bond, Martin. *A Dorset Family.* (Published privately).

Hutchins, John. 1774. *The History and Antiquities of the County of Dorset.*
EP Publishing in collaboration with Dorset County Library.

Kelly's Directory. 1923. London: Kelly & Co. Ltd.

Knight, Fred. 1994. *The Rooks in the Elm Trees.*
Wareham: Myrmica Books.

Legg, Rodney. 1998. *Tyneham, Ghost Village.*
Wincanton: Dorset Publishing Company.

Leighton, Brian. *A Short History of Tyneham.*
Bovington: Media Support Wing, RAC Centre, Allenby Barracks.

Lewer, David and Dennis Smale. 1994. *Swanage Past.*
Chichester: Phillimore.

Mansel, JC. 1967. *Kimmeridge, Smedmore and The Bay.*
Bournemouth: Anglebury Press.

Morris, Christopher. 1982. *The Illustrated Journeys of Celia Fiennes: 1685-1712.* Cresset Press.

Dorset Echo.

Dorset Magazine.

Dorset Record Office: *Tyneham National School Log Book: 1914-1942*; *Tyneham Parish Registers*; *Tyneham Church Monumental Inscriptions.*